Cherry Blossoms & Flowers of Japan Photobook

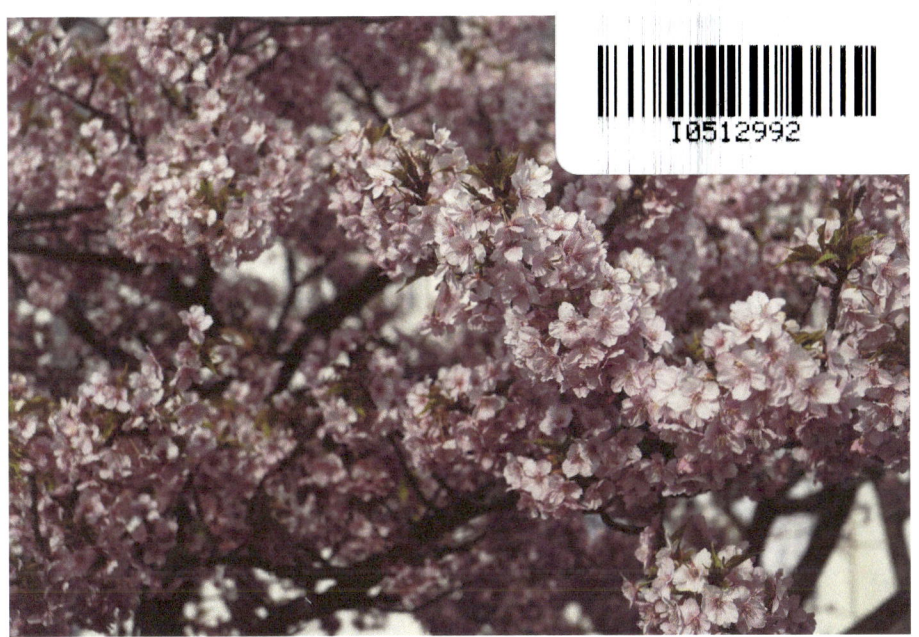

By Paul Su

Copyright © 2023 by Paul Su

All rights reserved.

No portion of this book may be reproduced in any form without written permission from the publisher or author, except as permitted by U.S. copyright law.

This publication is designed to provide accurate and authoritative information in regard to the subject matter covered. It is sold with the understanding that neither the author nor the publisher is engaged in rendering legal, investment, accounting or other professional services. While the publisher and author have used their best efforts in preparing this book, they make no representations or warranties with respect to the accuracy or completeness of the contents of this book and specifically disclaim any implied warranties of merchantability or fitness for a particular purpose. No warranty may be created or extended by sales representatives or written sales materials. The advice and strategies contained herein may not be suitable for your situation. You should consult with a professional when appropriate. Neither the publisher nor the author shall be liable for any loss of profit or any other commercial damages, including but not limited to special, incidental, consequential, personal, or other damages.

Book Cover by Paul Su
Photos by Paul Su
1st edition 2023

Social Media Sites (SNS)

YouTube: https://www.youtube.com/c/TokyoPaulLive
Instagram: https://www.instagram.com/tokyopaullive
Twitter: https://twitter.com/tokyopaullive
Facebook:
https://www.facebook.com/groups/tokyopaul (groups)
https://www.facebook.com/TheTokyoPaul (page)

Acknowledgements

I want to convey my sincere appreciation to the viewers of my YouTube channel Tokyo Paul, who gave me support and motivation when I was working on this project. This book would not have been possible without their support.

I also like to express my gratitude to my wife for her help. Her invaluable feedback and support were essential in making this idea a success.

I want to thank my family, friends, and readers again for their kindness and support. Thank you to everyone from the bottom of my heart.

Kawazu Early Cherry Blossoms

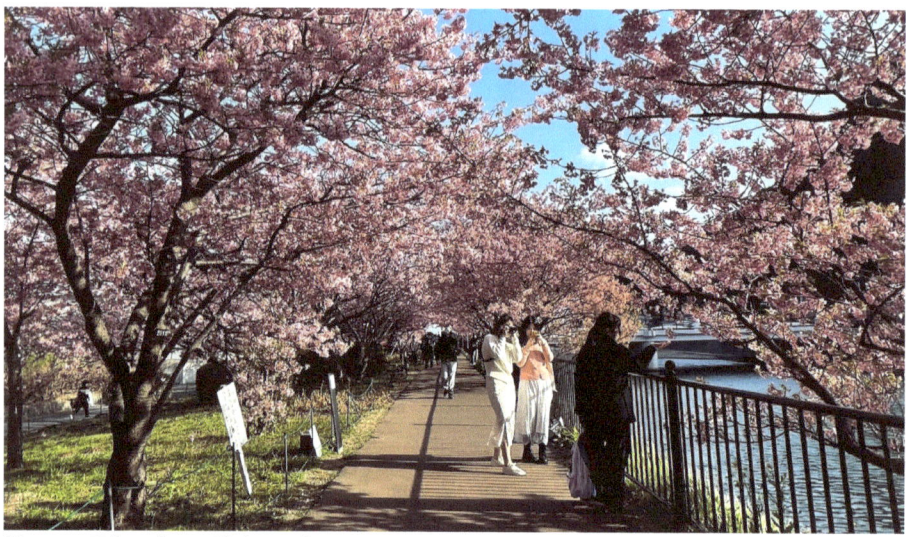

Kamo District, Shizuoka Japan

Description:

The Kawazu Cherry Blossoms are a breathtaking display of nature's beauty, located in the town of Kawazu, Japan, and known for their early blooming season, often appearing as early as late January or early February, attracting visitors from all over to see the delicate pink and white flowers in full bloom.

Kawazu Early Cherry Blossoms

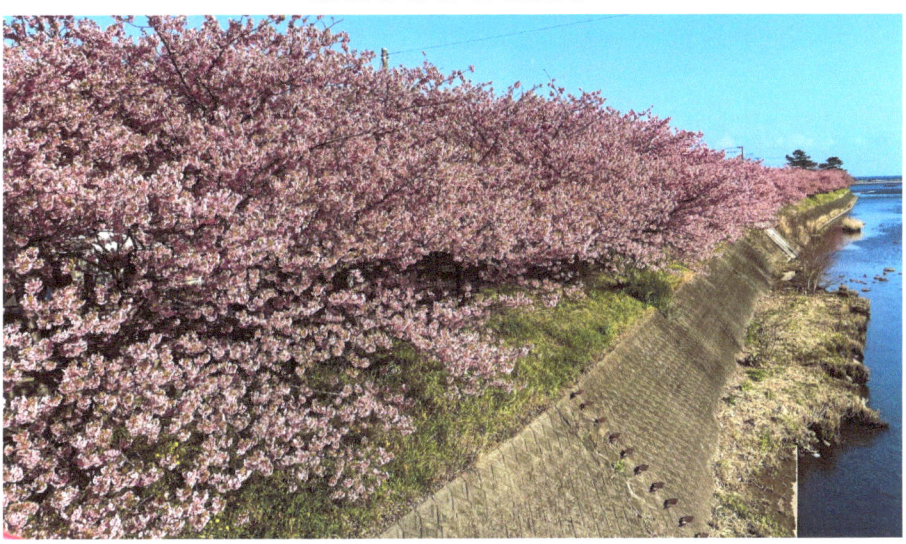

Kamo District, Shizuoka Japan

Description:

Visitors can marvel at the stunning cherry blossoms against the backdrop of the nearby mountains and sea.

Kawazu Early Cherry Blossoms

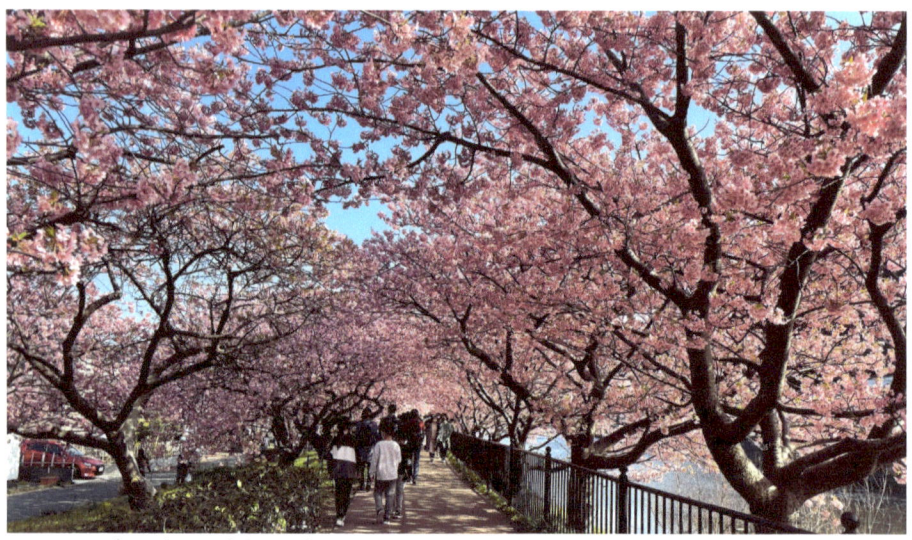

Kamo District, Shizuoka Japan

Description:

The Kawazu Cherry Blossoms are a popular tourist and local attraction.

Kawazu Early Cherry Blossoms

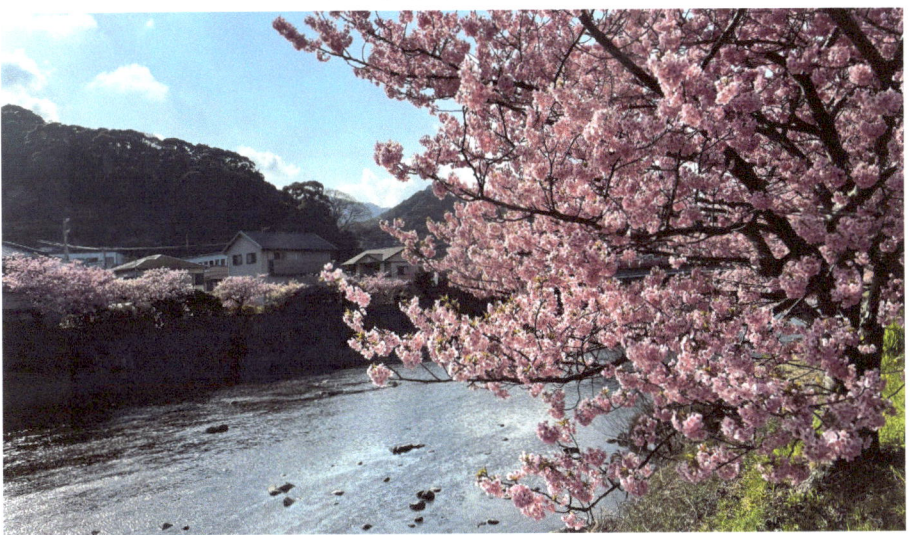

Kamo District, Shizuoka Japan

Description:
Kawazu Cherry Blossoms have a short blooming period, lasting only a few weeks.

Kairakuen Garden

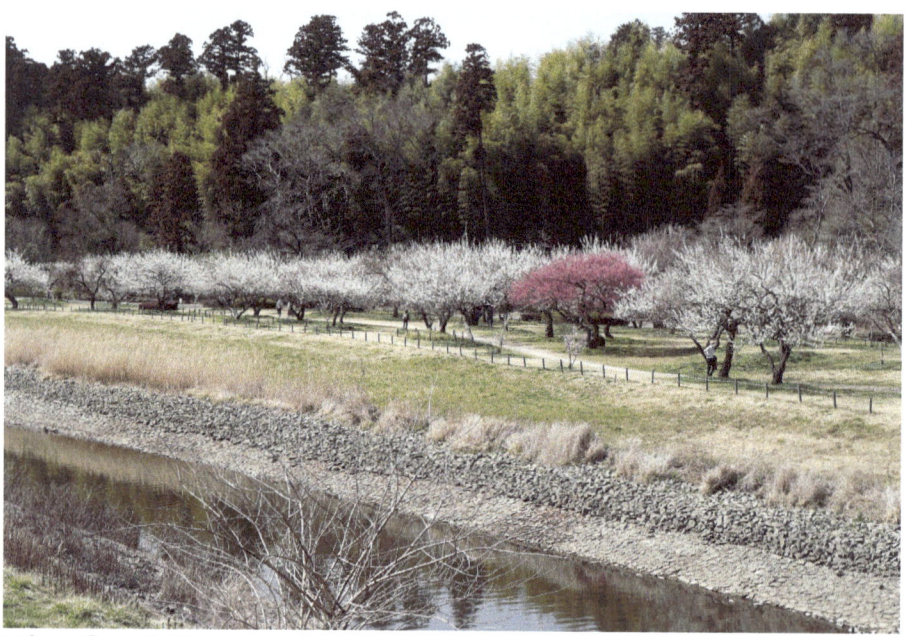

Mito, Ibaraki Japan

Description:
The garden is a must-see for nature and garden enthusiasts, providing a peaceful relief from city life.

Kairakuen Garden

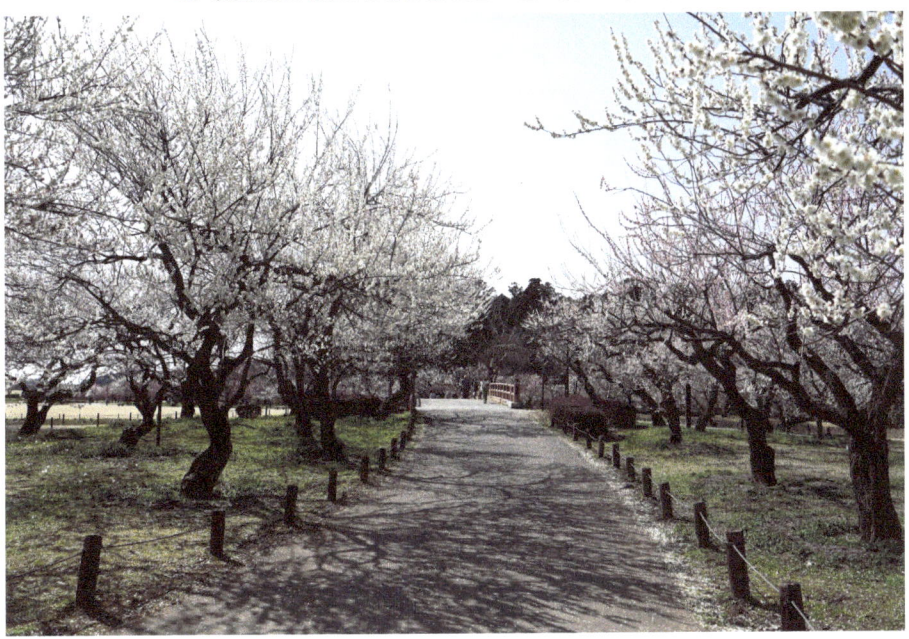

Mito, Ibaraki Japan

Description:
The garden is famous for its plum blossoms, which bloom in the early spring.

Kairakuen Garden

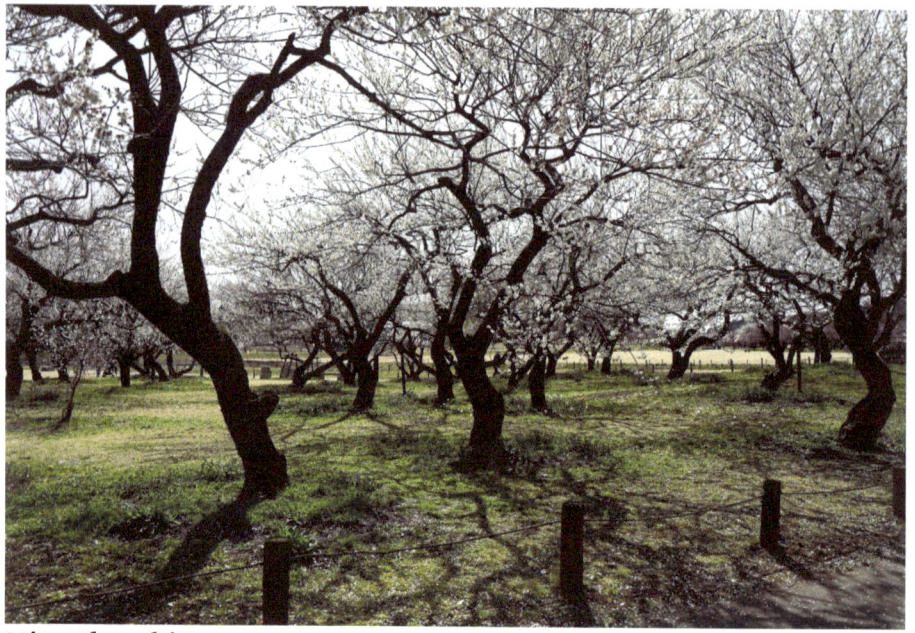

Mito, Ibaraki Japan

Description:
The garden is open all year and features seasonal attractions throughout the year.

Kairakuen Garden

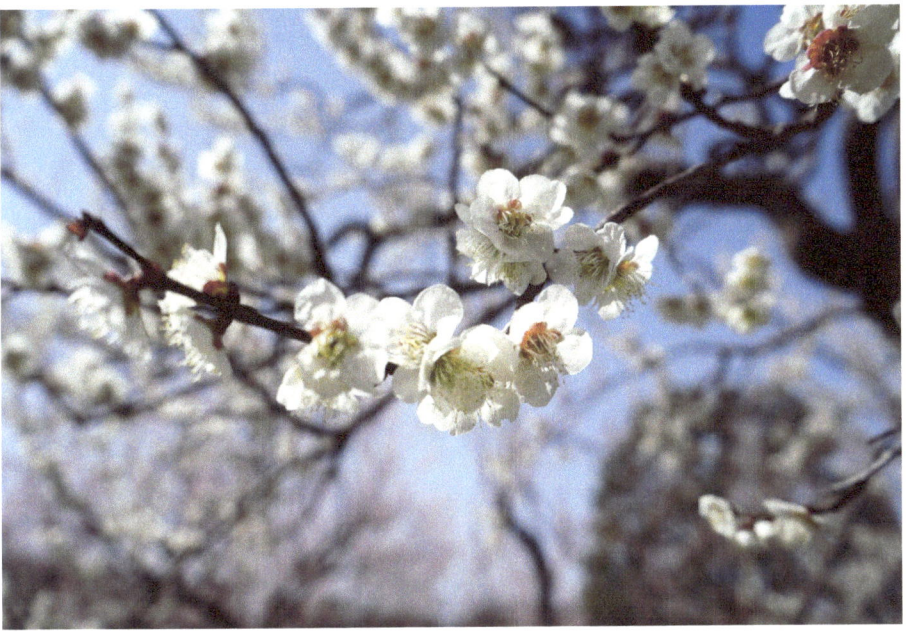

Mito, Ibaraki Japan

Description:

Kairakuen Garden is a large park with more than 3,000 plum and cherry blossom trees.

Kairakuen Garden

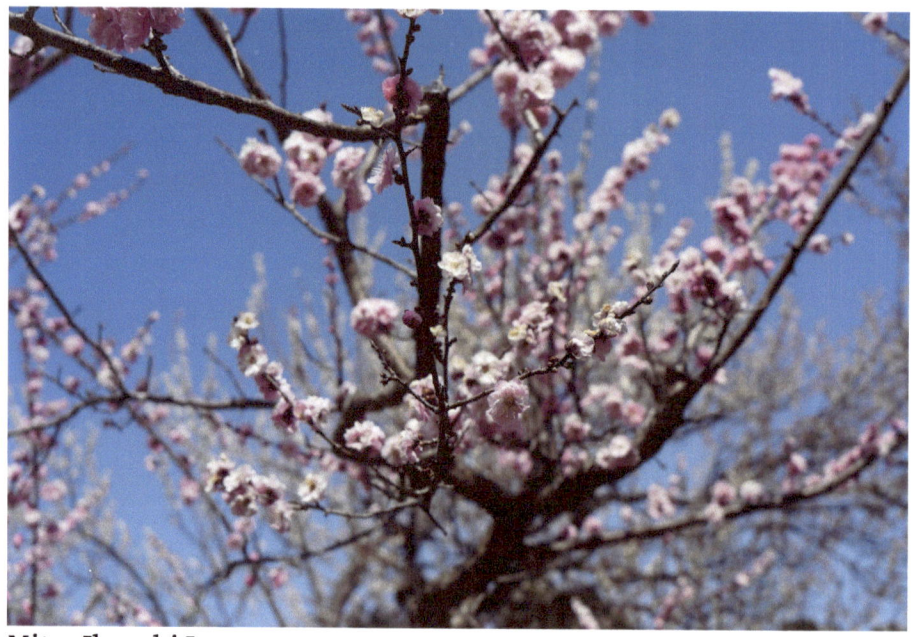

Mito, Ibaraki Japan

Description:
The garden is well-known for its plum trees, which bloom in February and early March.

Kairakuen Garden

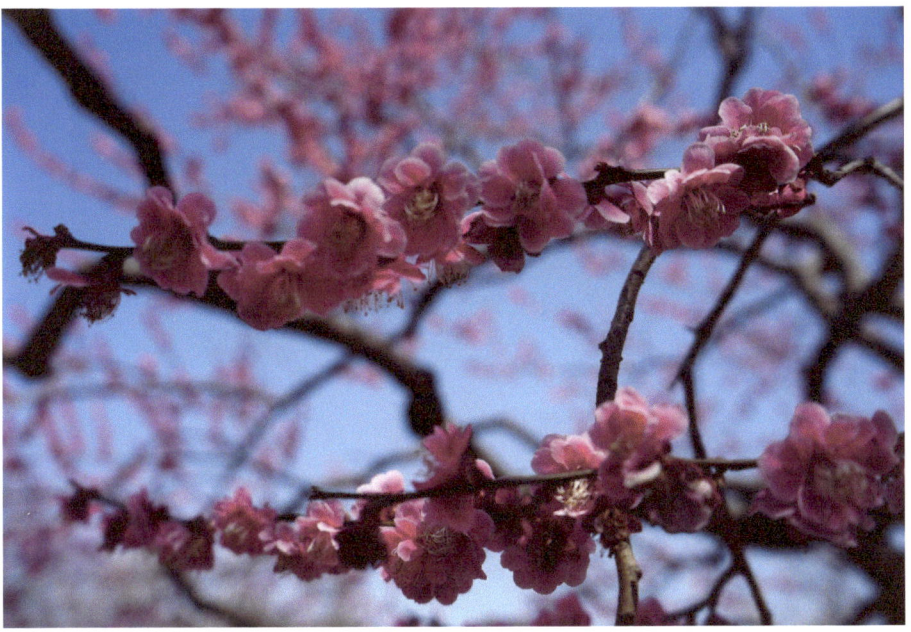

Mito, Ibaraki Japan

Description:
The garden was originally built in the early nineteenth century by the local lord Tokugawa Nariaki.

Kairakuen Garden

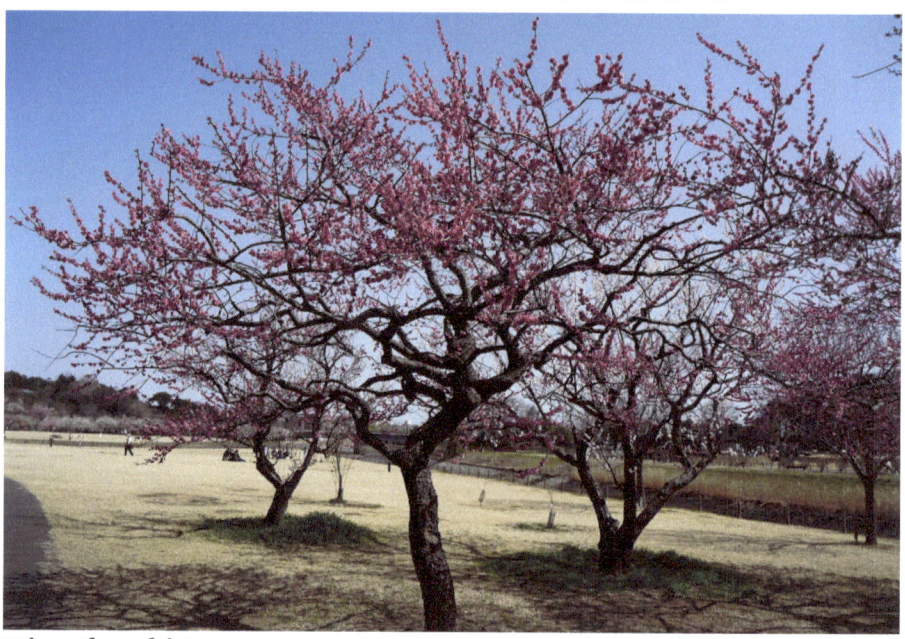

Mito, Ibaraki Japan

Description:

The garden is easily accessible from Tokyo by train or car, making it an ideal day trip destination.

Kairakuen Garden

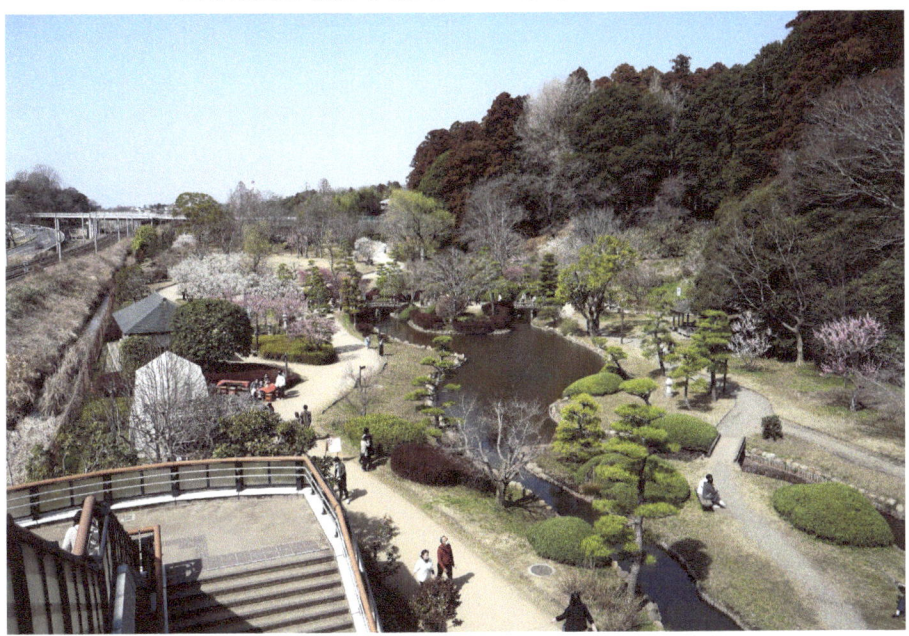

Mito, Ibaraki Japan

Description:

The garden is one of Japan's Three Great Gardens, along with Kenrokuen in Kanazawa and Korakuen in Okayama.

Kairakuen Garden

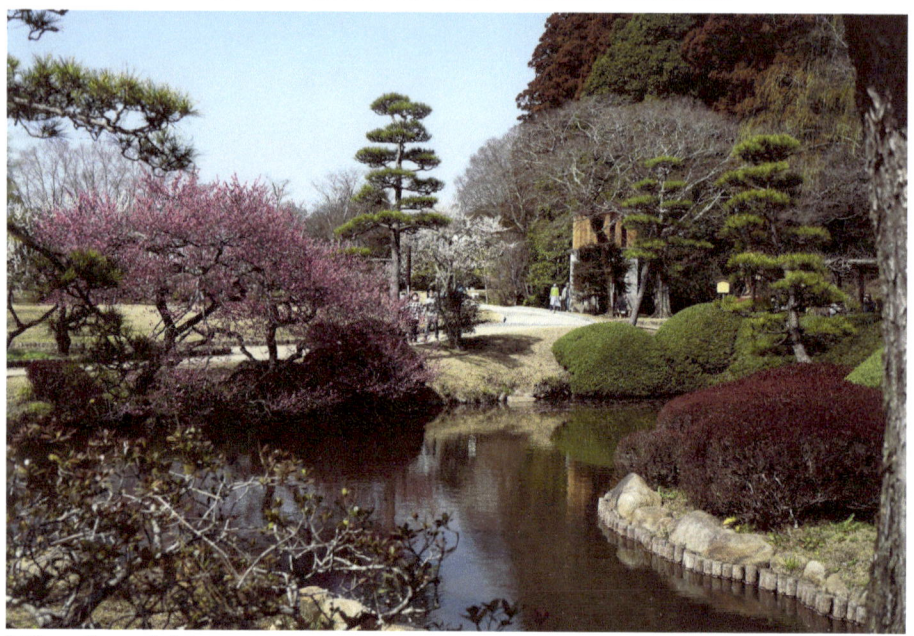

Mito, Ibaraki Japan

Description:

Kairakuen Garden is regarded as one of Japan's most beautiful gardens and is a must-see for nature lovers.

Kairakuen Garden

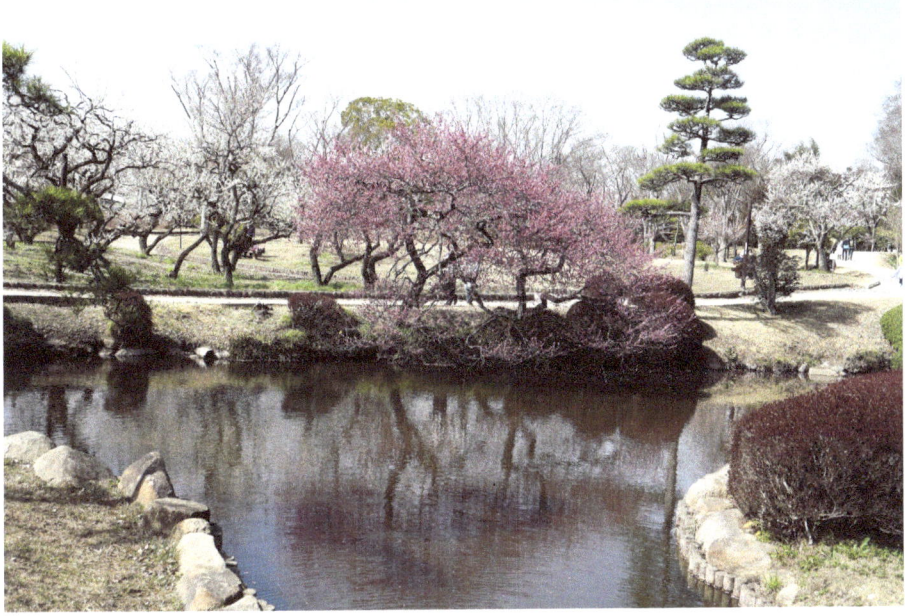

Mito, Ibaraki Japan

Description:
Kairakuen Garden is regarded as one of Japan's most beautiful gardens and is a must-see for nature lovers.

Kairakuen Kobuntei-House

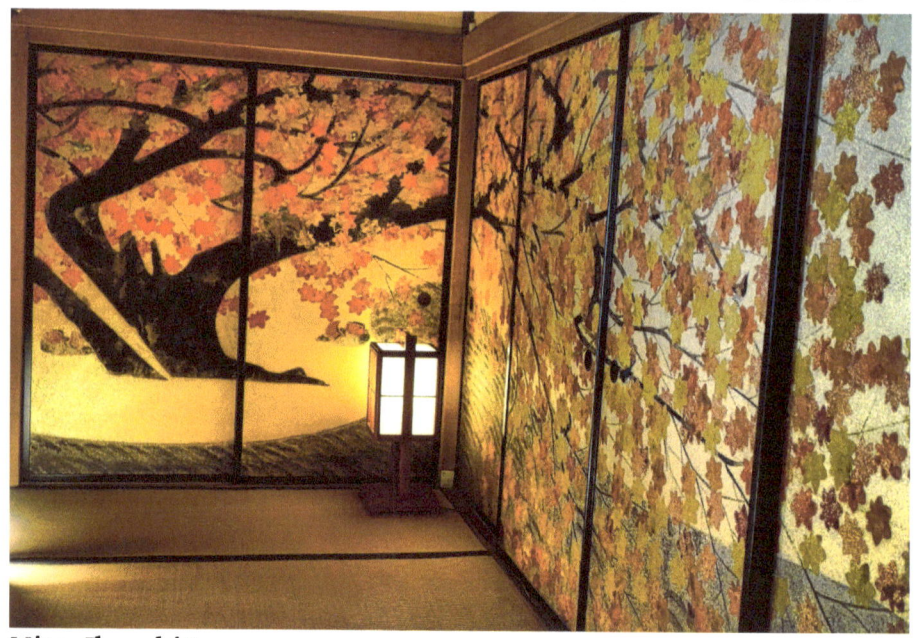

Mito, Ibaraki Japan

Description:
Nariaki Tokugawa designed Kobuntei as a resting place in the garden.

Kairakuen Kobuntei- House View

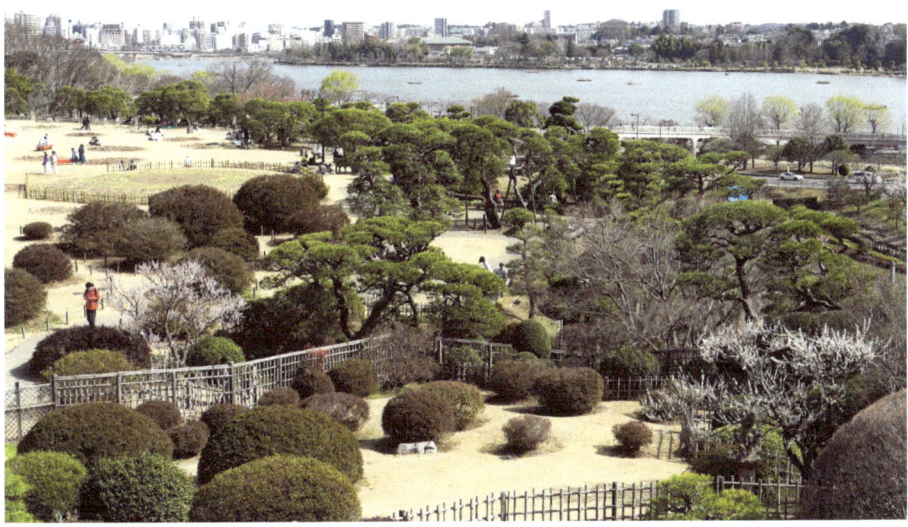

Mito, Ibaraki Japan

Description:
The park is also well-known for its stunning views of the nearby mountains and landscape.

Hakusan Shrine Hydrangea Festival

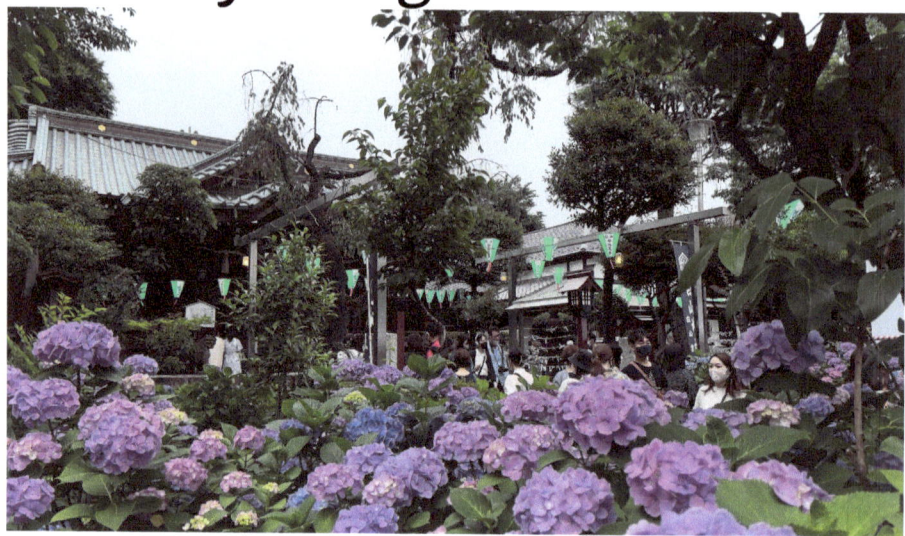

Bunkyo City, Tokyo Japan

Description:

The Hakusan Shrine Hydrangea Festival is a lovely celebration of hydrangea blooming in Japan.

Hakusan Shrine Hydrangea Festival

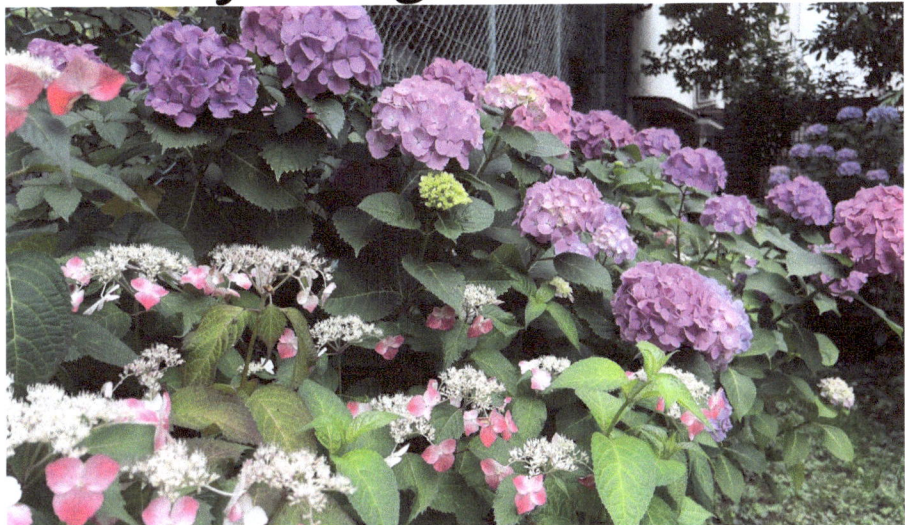

Bunkyo City, Tokyo Japan

Description:

At the festival, visitors can marvel at the sight of thousands of colorful hydrangea flowers in full bloom. This annual event held in June attracts both tourists and locals, providing a unique and memorable experience.

Nezu Shrine

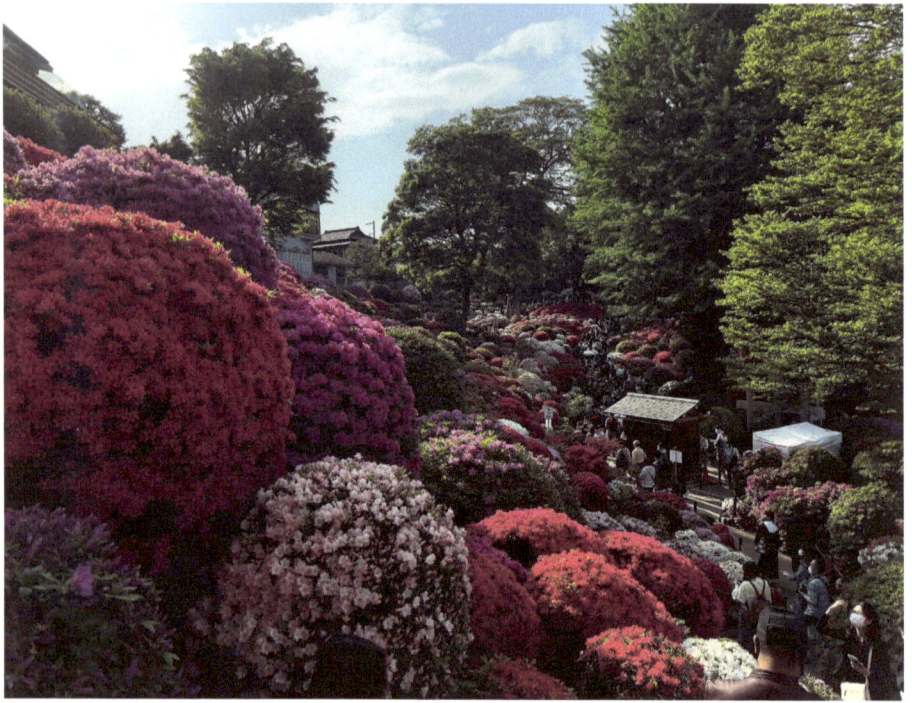

Bunkyo City, Tokyo Japan

Description:

The Nezu Shrine Hydrangea Festival is a must-see event in Tokyo for nature lovers.

Nezu Shrine

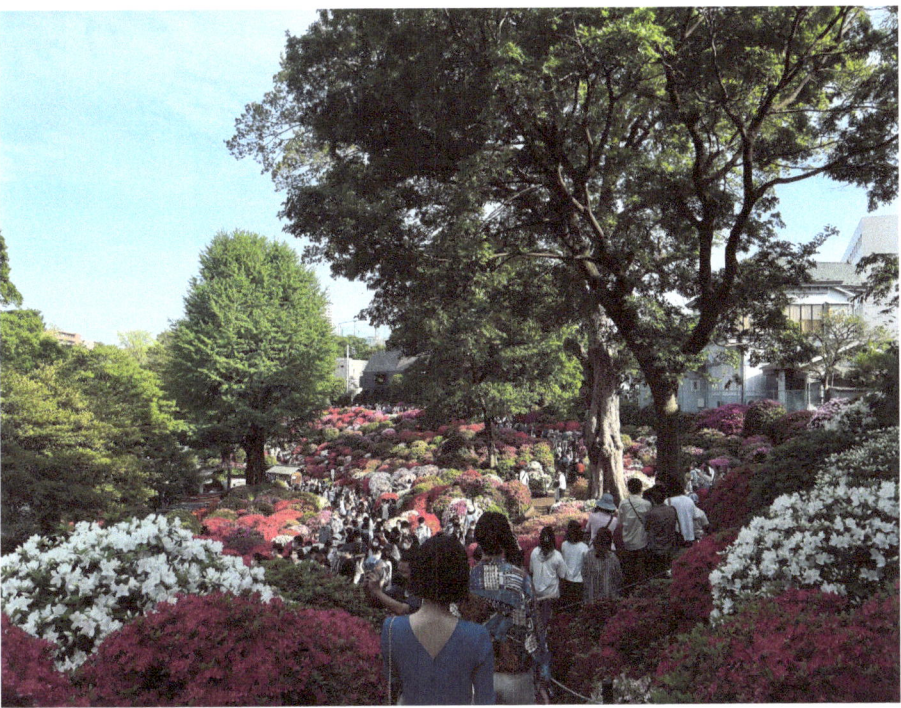

Bunkyo City, Tokyo Japan
Description:
Over 3,000 vibrant hydrangea plants are on display at the festival, creating a stunning display of colors and textures. At the festival, visitors can also enjoy traditional Japanese performances and delicious food stalls.

Sagamiko

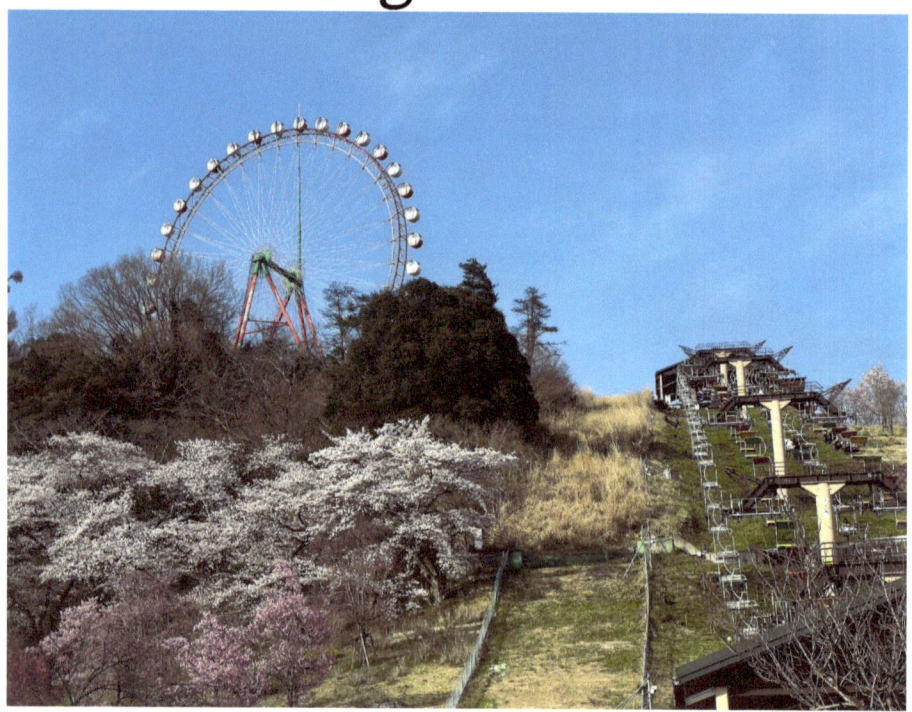

Sagamihara, Kanagawa, Japan

Description:

The Sagamiko Blossoms are part of the Sagamiko Resort Pleasure Forest in Kanagawa prefecture.

Sagamiko

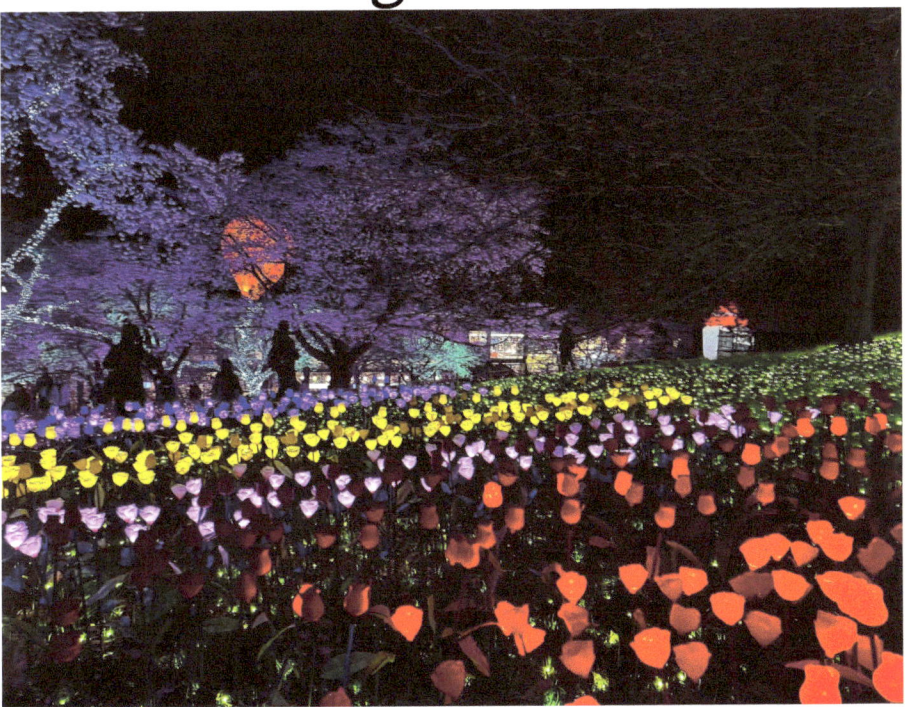

Sagamihara, Kanagawa, Japan

Description:

The flowers are frequently illuminated at night, creating a romantic and magical atmosphere.

Evening Cherry Blossoms

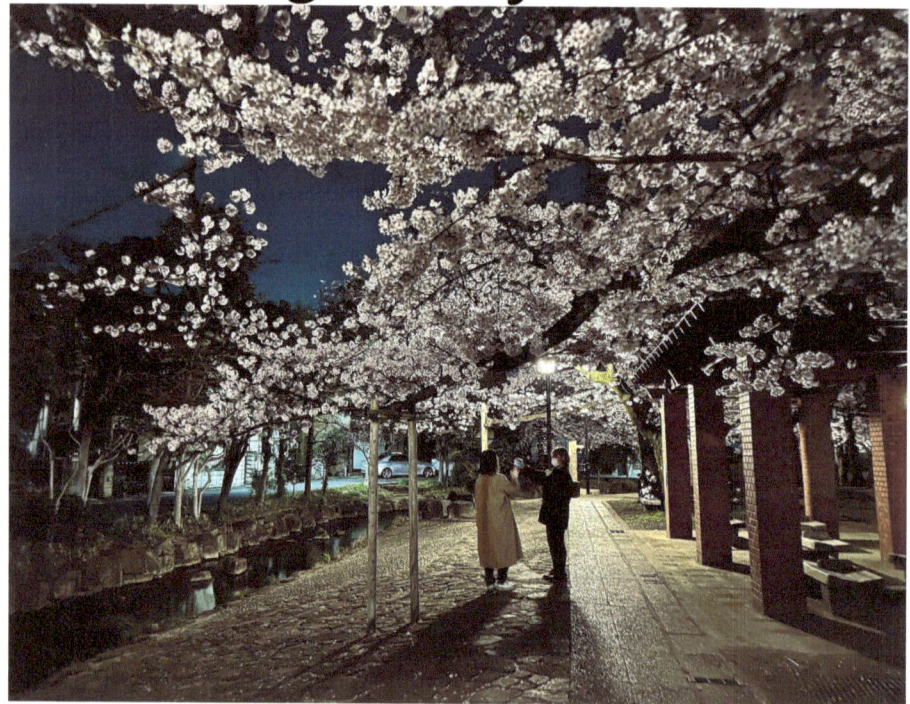

Edogawaku, Tokyo, Japan

Description:
The Edogawaku Cherry Blossoms typically bloom from late March to early April.

Spring Cherry Blossoms Meguro

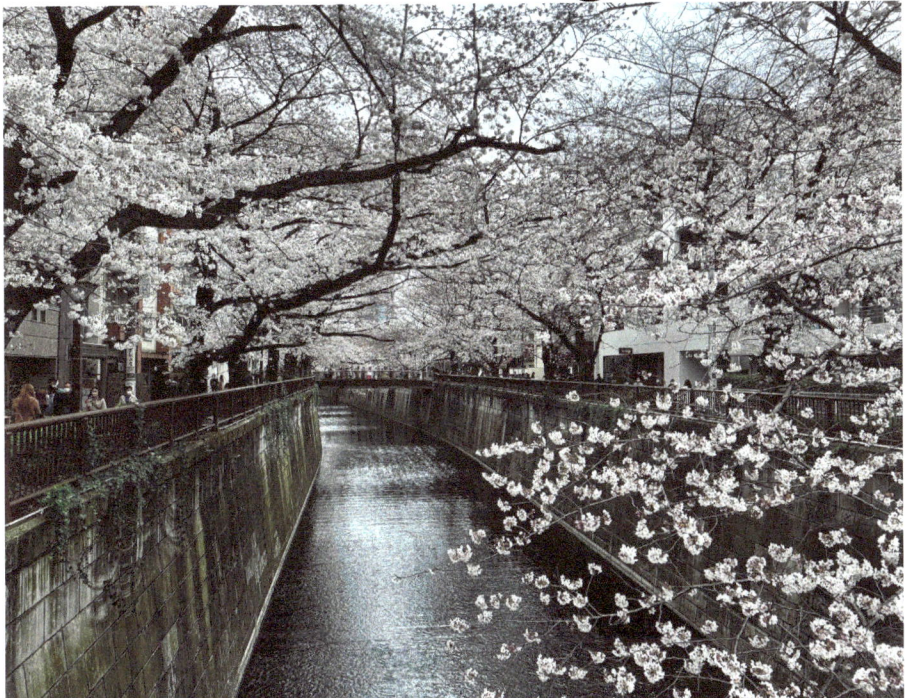

Meguro City, Tokyo Japan

Description:
The cherry blossom trees that line the banks of the Meguro River create a lovely and peaceful atmosphere.

Cherry Blossoms

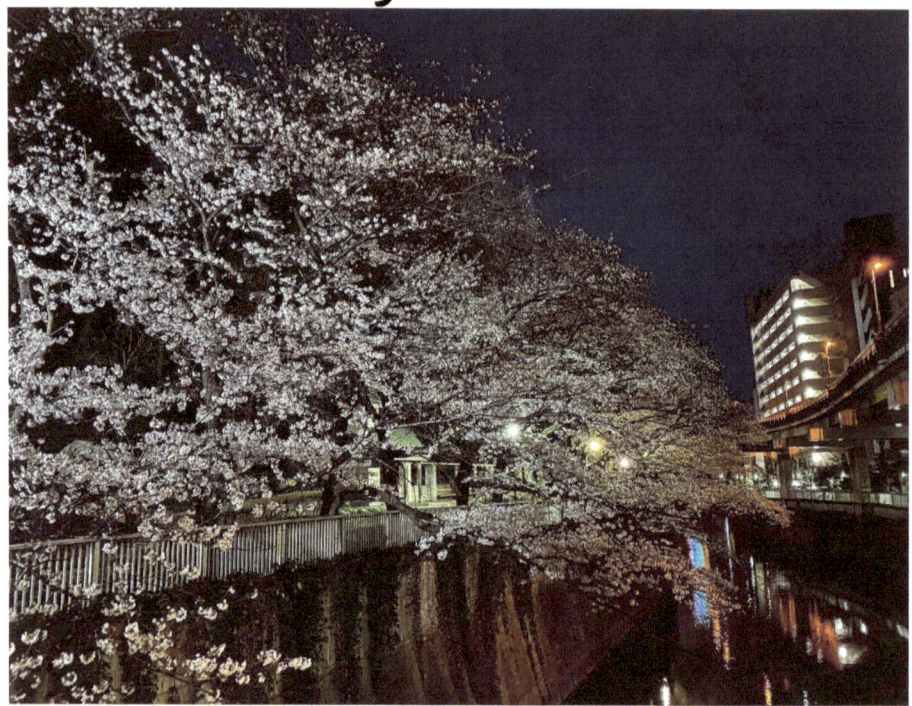

Edogawa, Tokyo, Japan

Description:
The cherry trees are illuminated at night, creating a completely different and equally beautiful experience.

Cherry Blossoms

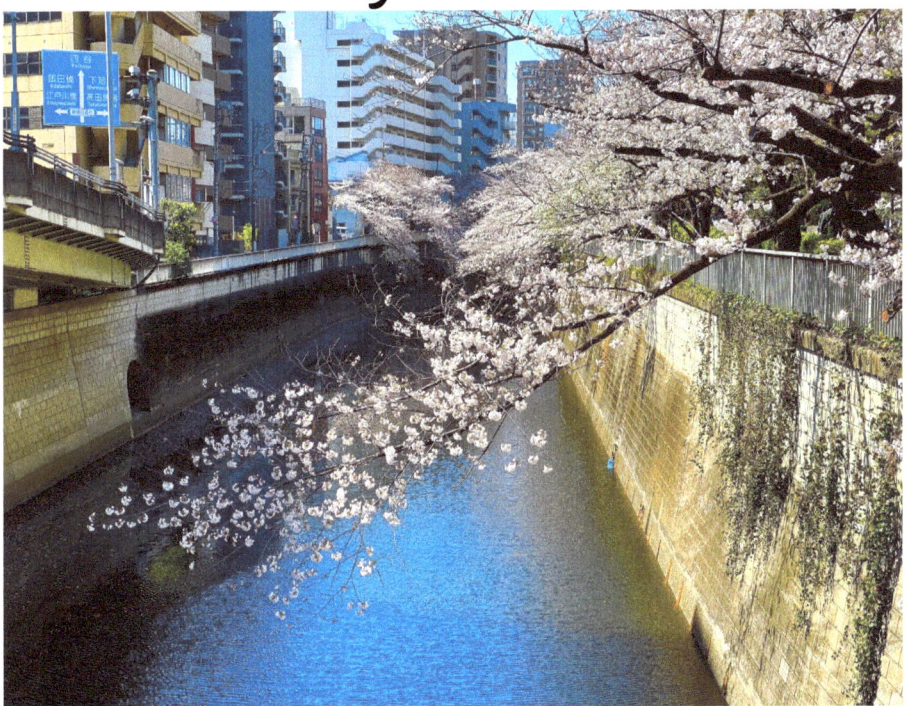

Edogawa, Tokyo, Japan

Description:

The Edogawa Park Cherry Blossoms are located in Tokyo's Edogawa Ward. Over 1,000 cherry blossom trees dot the park, creating a stunning pink canopy.

Showa Kinen Park

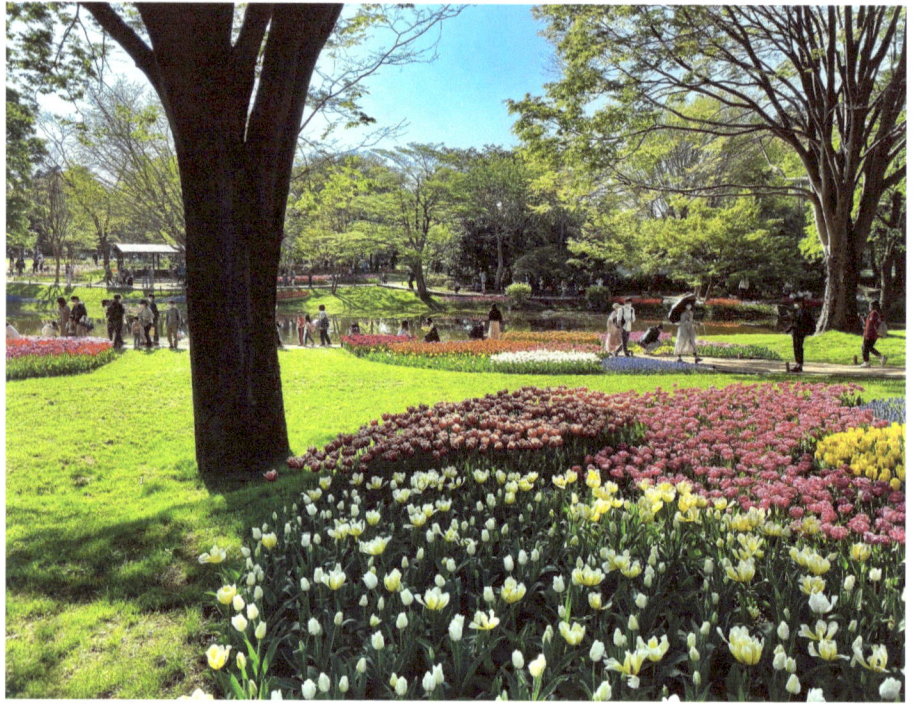

Tachikawa, Tokyo, Japan

Description:
Tachikawa, Tokyo, hosts the Showa Kinden Park Tulip Festival.

Showa Kinen Park

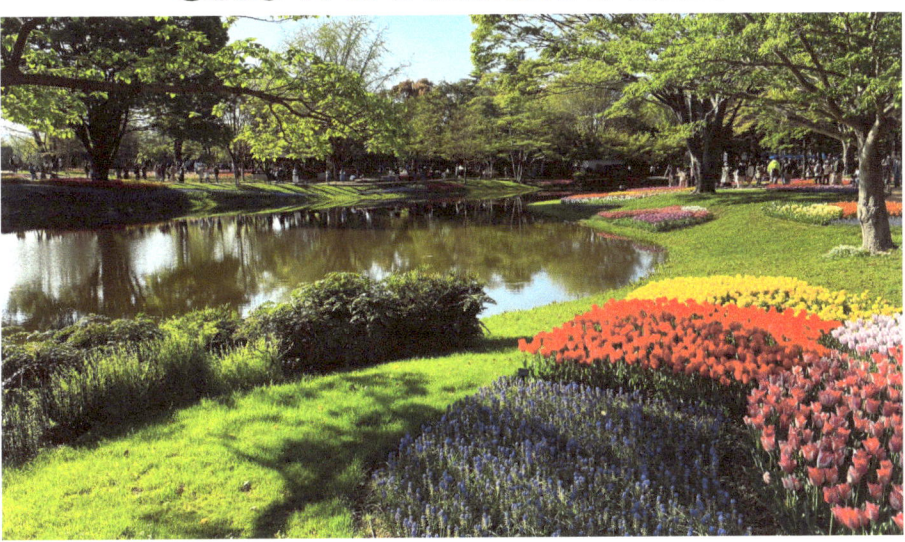

Tachikawa, Tokyo, Japan

Description:
Over 300,000 tulips of various colors and varieties are on display at the festival.

Tokyo Station Cherry Blossoms Fall

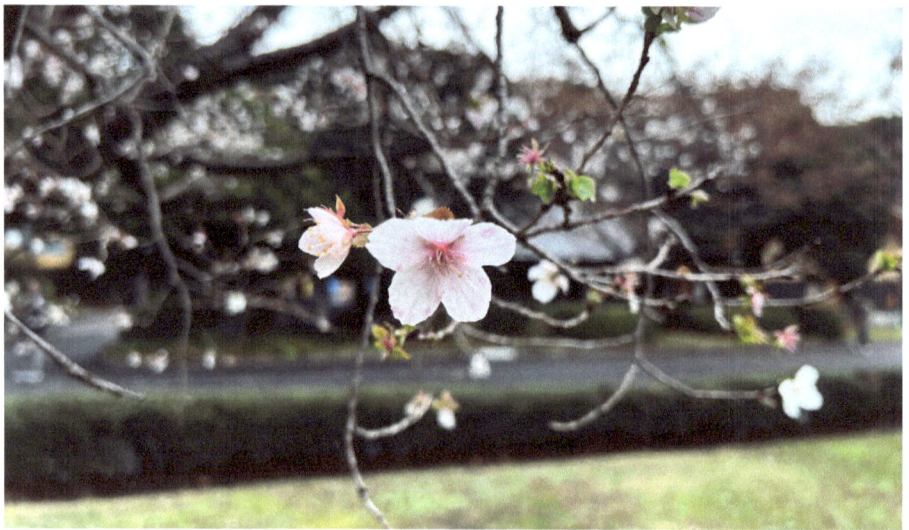

Tokyo, Japan

Description:

The Cherry Blossoms in Tokyo Station are a popular location for viewing cherry blossoms in the heart of Tokyo.

Roppongi Evening Cherry Blossoms

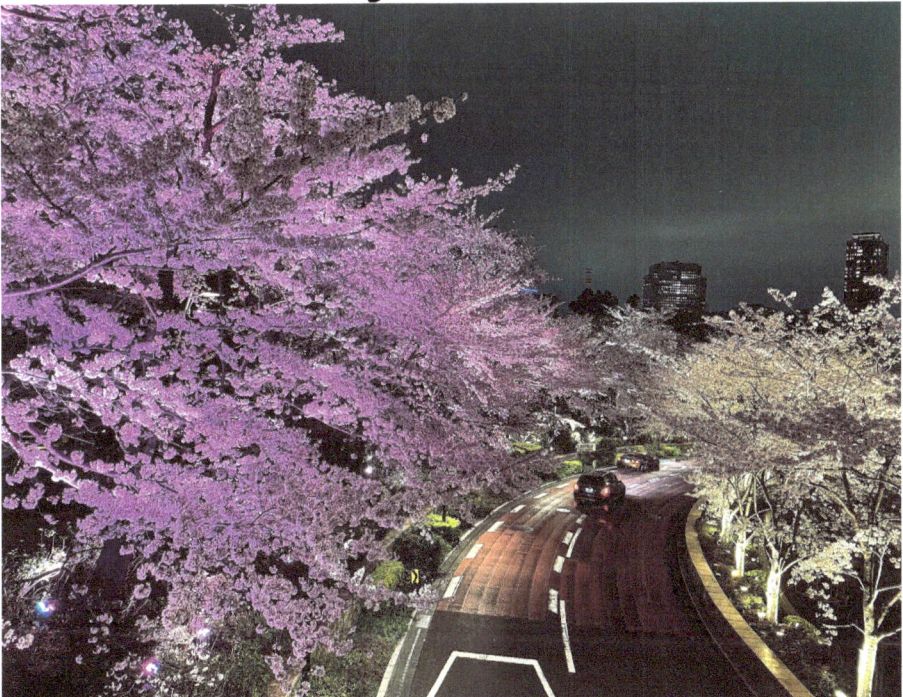

Tokyo Japan

Description:
The cherry trees are frequently illuminated at night, creating a romantic and magical atmosphere.

Meguro Cherry Blossoms

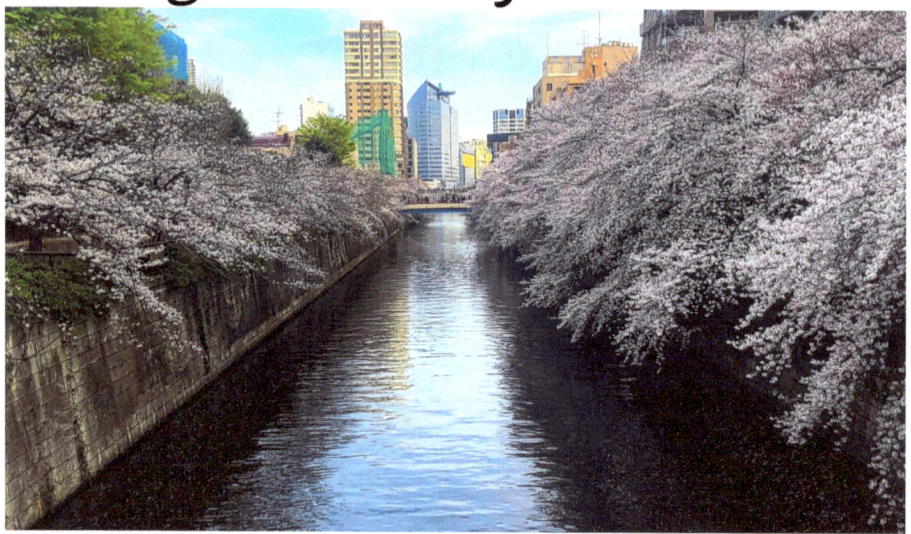

Meguro City, Tokyo, Japan

Description:

The area is a popular spot for cherry blossom viewing and taking leisurely strolls along the river.

Kochia Hill In Hitachinaka

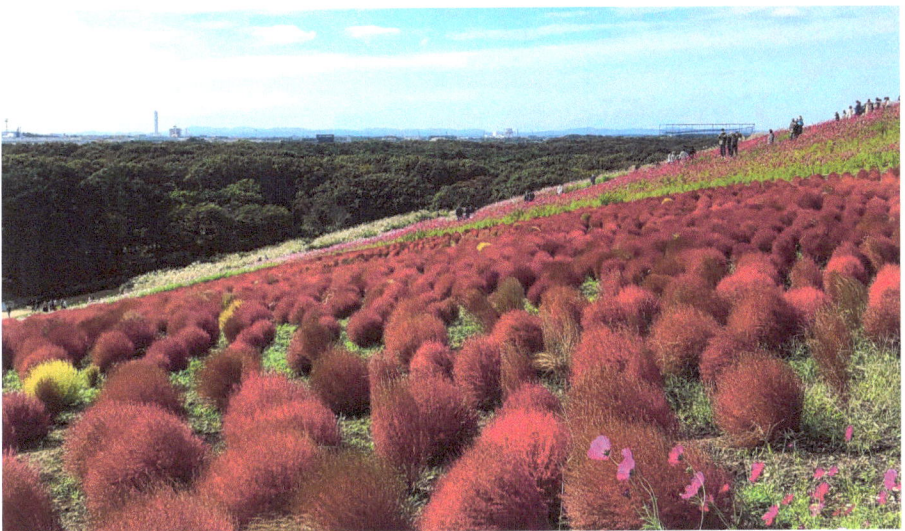

Ibaraki, Hitachinaka, Japan

Description:
The park is well-known for its beautiful seasonal flower displays, which include tulips, nemophila, and, of course, cherry blossoms.

Hibiya Park

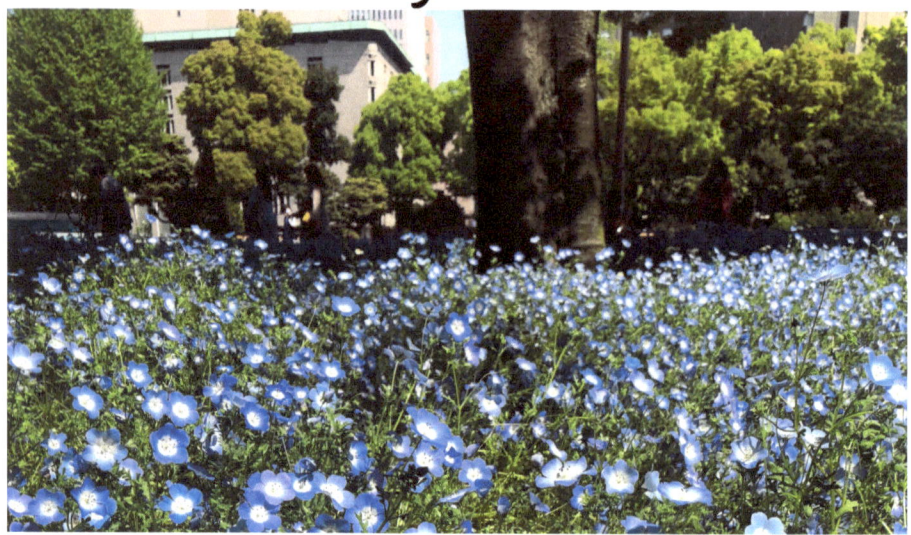

Tokyo, Japan

Description:

With over 300 cherry blossom trees, the park is a popular spot for cherry blossom viewing.

Ashikaga Flower Park

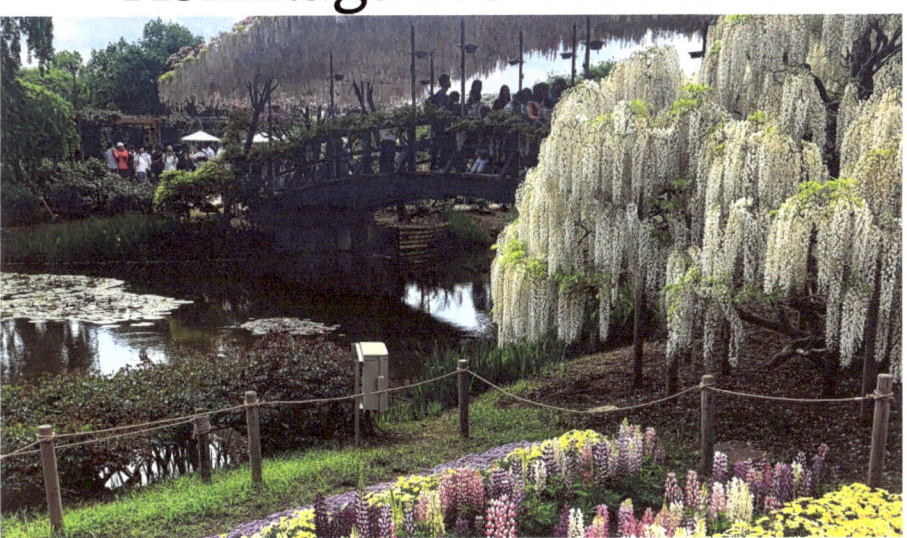

Ashikaga, Tochigi, Japan

Description:
The park is famous for its stunning displays of wisteria flowers in a variety of colors.

Ashikaga Flower Park

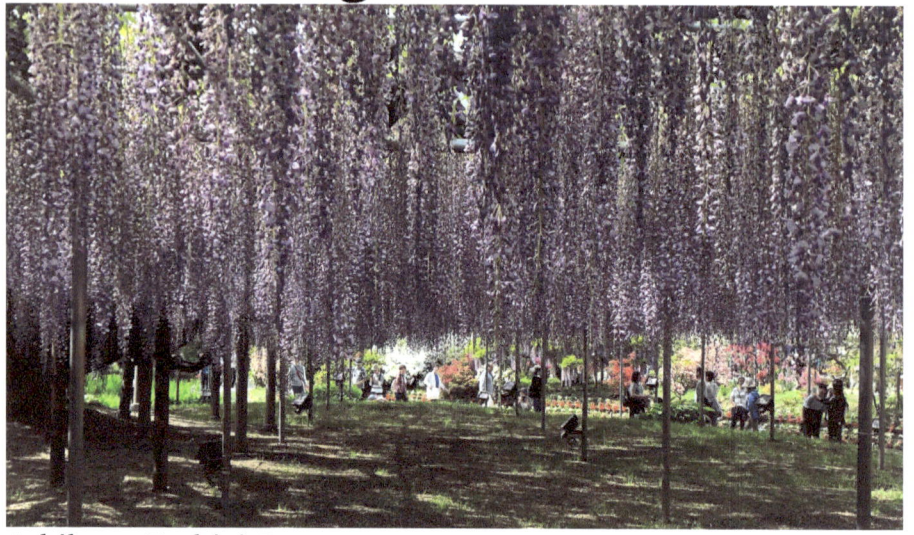

Ashikaga, Tochigi, Japan

Description:

The flowers are beautiful both during the day and at night, when they are beautifully illuminated.

Ashikaga Flower Park

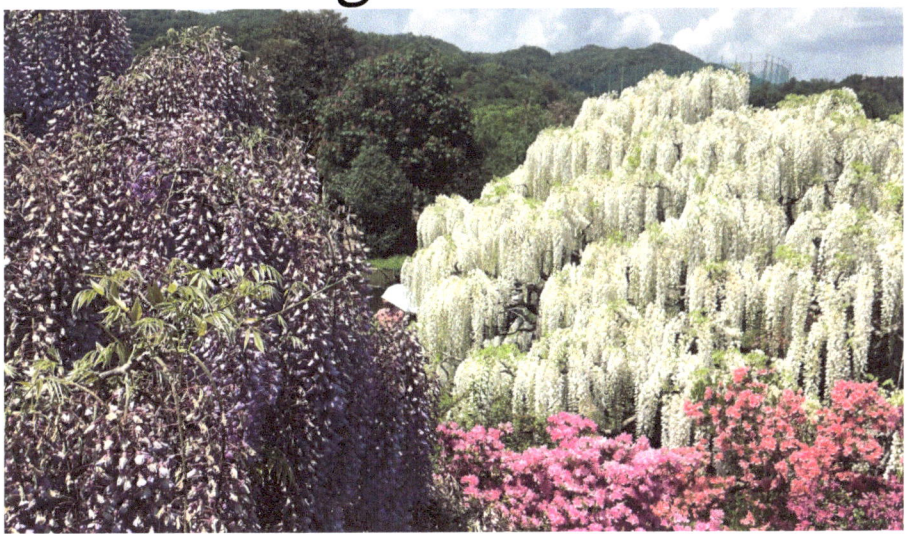

Ashikaga, Tochigi, Japan

Description:

Other seasonal flowers found in the park include roses, tulips, and cosmos.

Ashikaga Flower Park

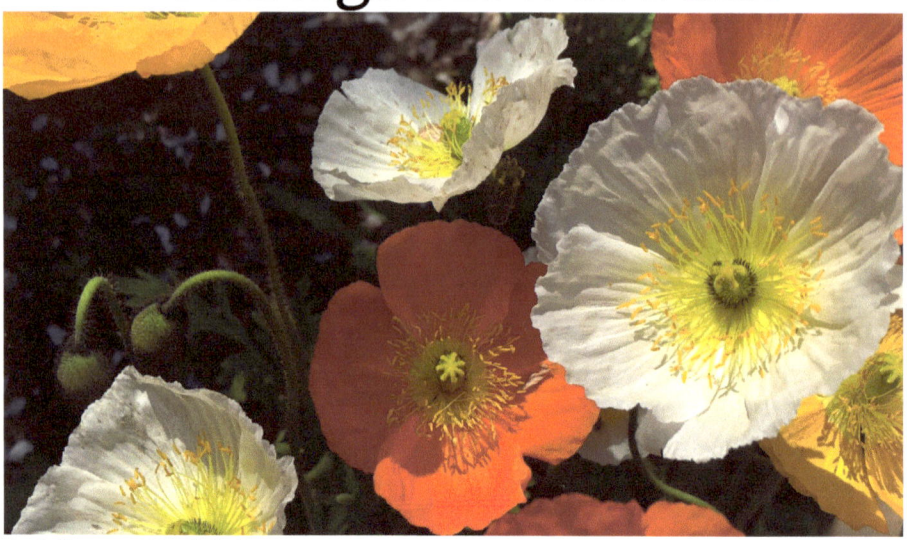

Ashikaga, Tochigi, Japan

Description:
Ashikaga Flower Park is located in Tochigi Prefecture, Japan.

Cherry Blossoms at Skytree Tower

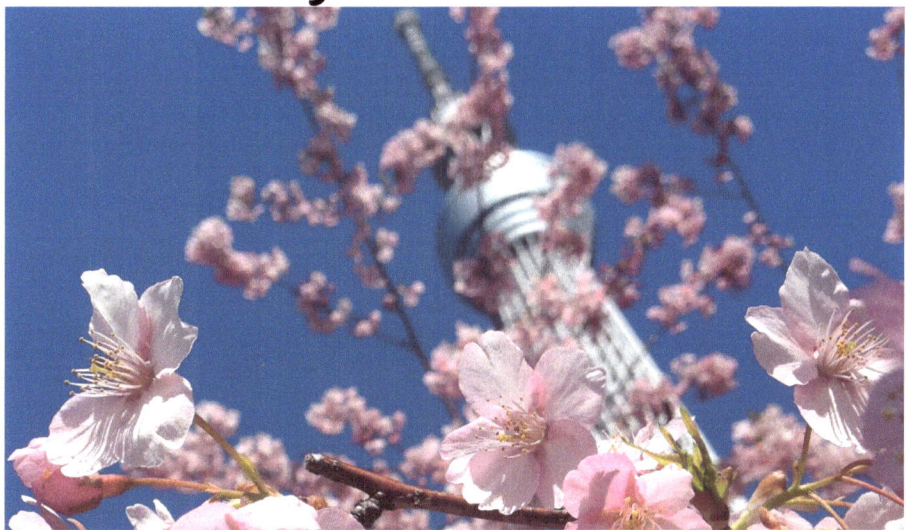

Tokyo, Japan

Description:
The sight of cherry blossoms against the backdrop of Tokyo's skyline is breathtaking.

Hirai Cherry Blossom

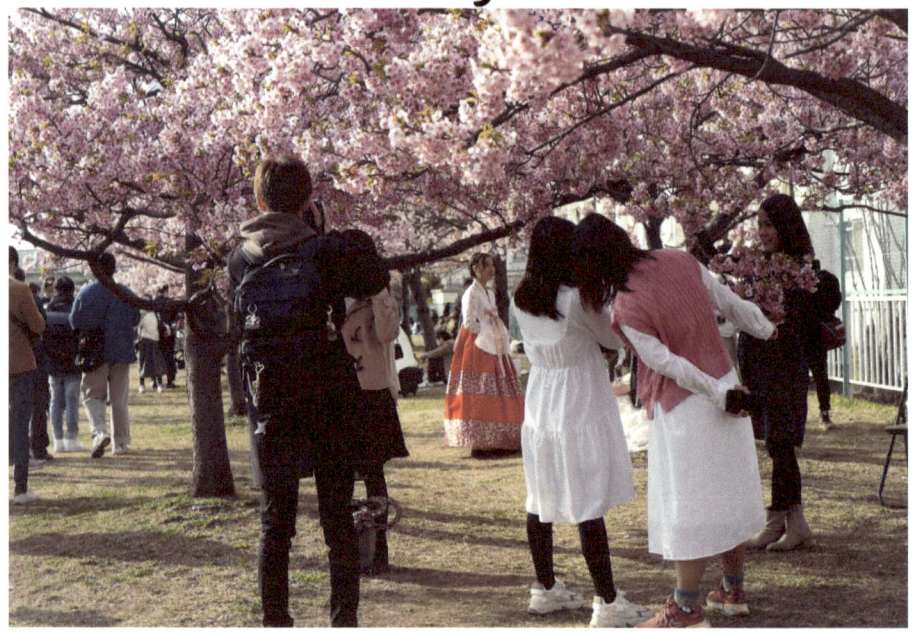

Edogawa City, Tokyo Japan

Description:
In the spring, the Hirai Cherry Blossoms are a sight to behold.

Hirai Cherry Blossom

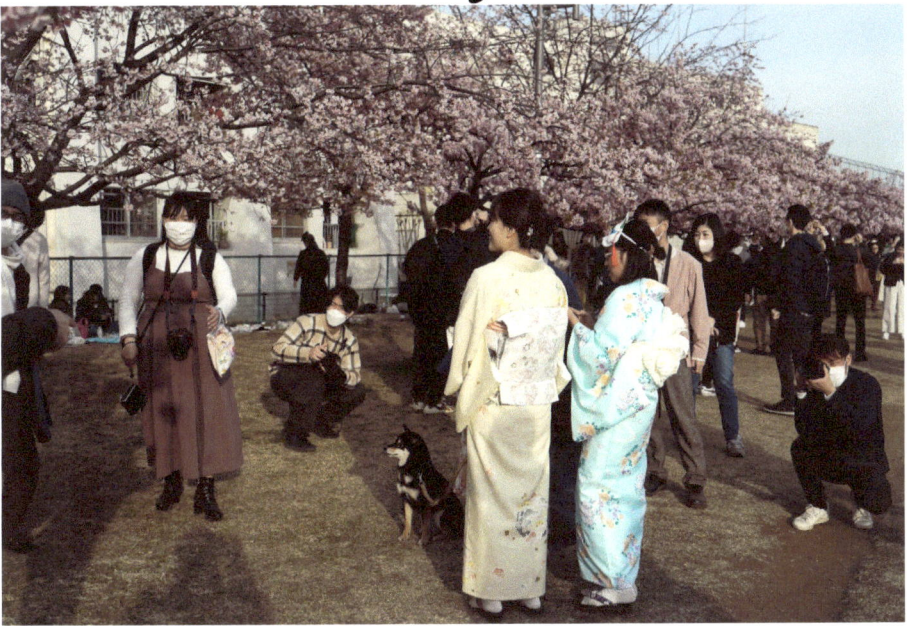

Edogawa City, Tokyo Japan

Description:

Depending on the weather, the blooming season lasts from late March to early April.

Hirai Cherry Blossom

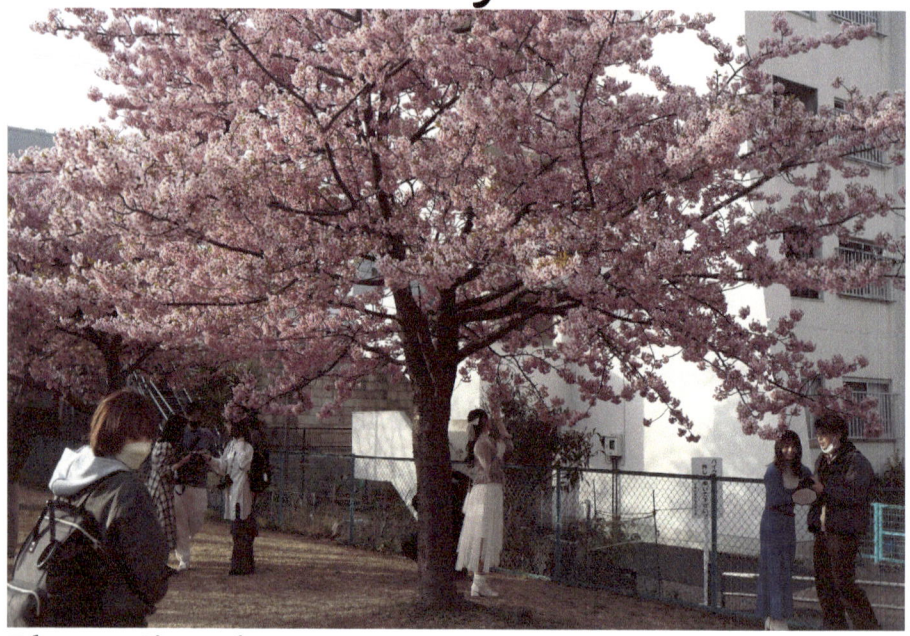

Edogawa City, Tokyo Japan

Description:
These cherry trees can be found in Tokyo's Hirai neighborhood.

Hirai Cherry Blossom

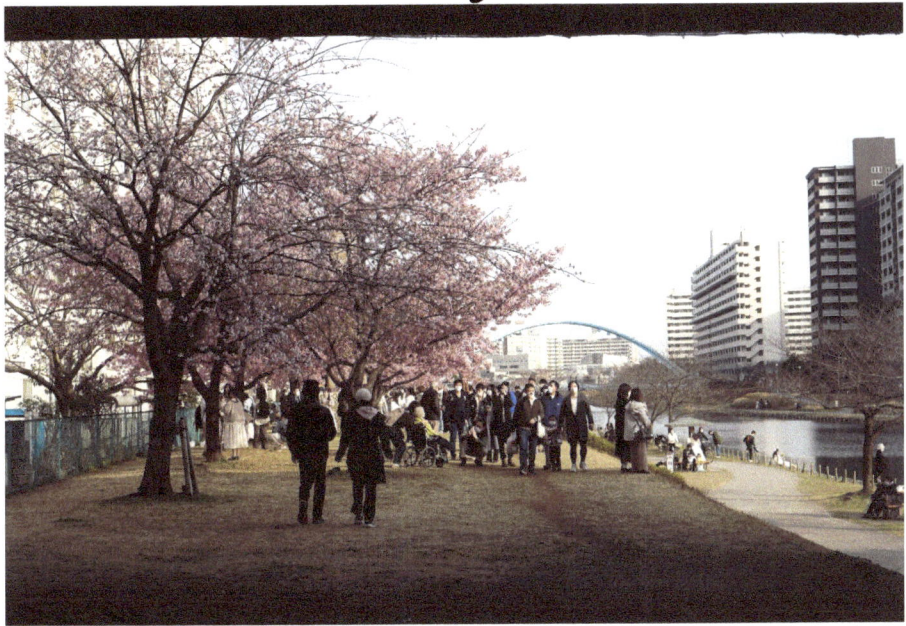

Edogawa City, Tokyo Japan

Description:

It's a popular spot for hanami, or cherry blossom viewing parties, for both locals and tourists.

Hirai Cherry Blossom

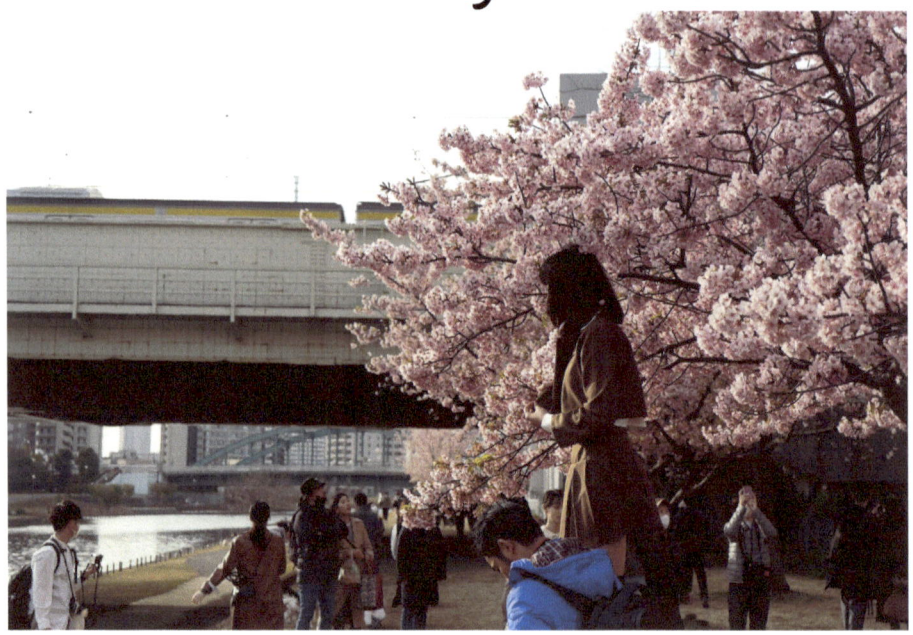

Edogawa City, Tokyo Japan

Description:

The fluffy and delicate pink petals of the Hirai Cherry Blossoms are particularly well-known.

Hirai Cherry Blossom

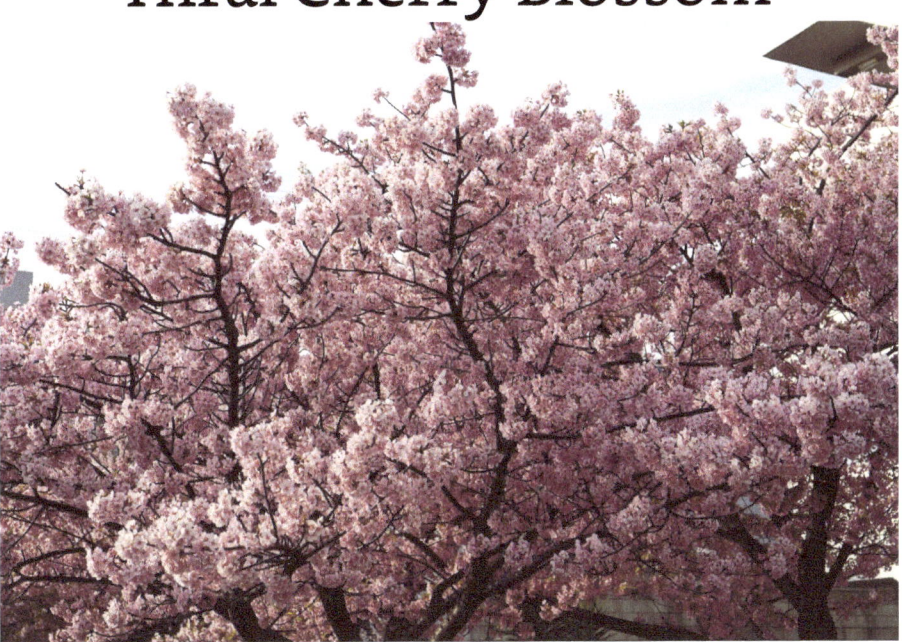

Edogawa City, Tokyo Japan

Description:

In Japan, the cherry blossom season is a significant event that symbolizes new beginnings and the fleeting nature of life.

Hirai Cherry Blossom

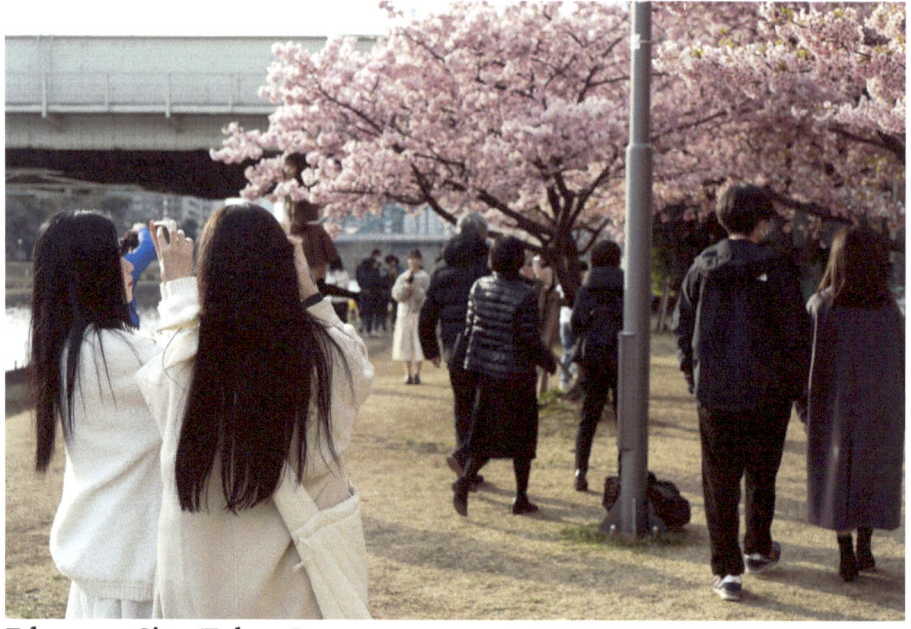

Edogawa City, Tokyo Japan

Description:

During the peak bloom season, the areas around the cherry trees are frequently crowded with excited visitors.

Hirai Cherry Blossom

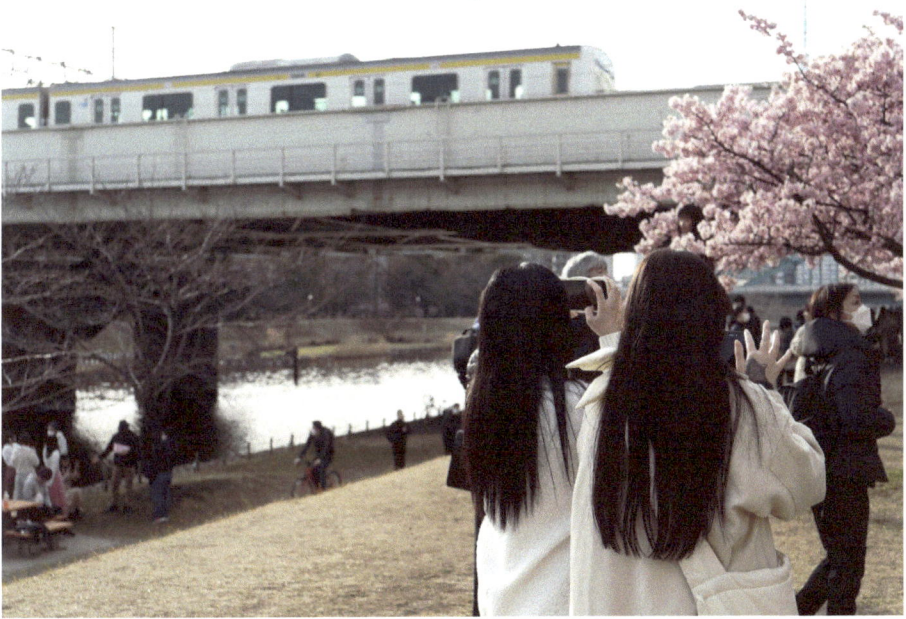

Edogawa City, Tokyo Japan

Description:
Visitors will find the Hirai area to be a convenient destination because it is easily accessible by public transportation.

Hirai Cherry Blossom

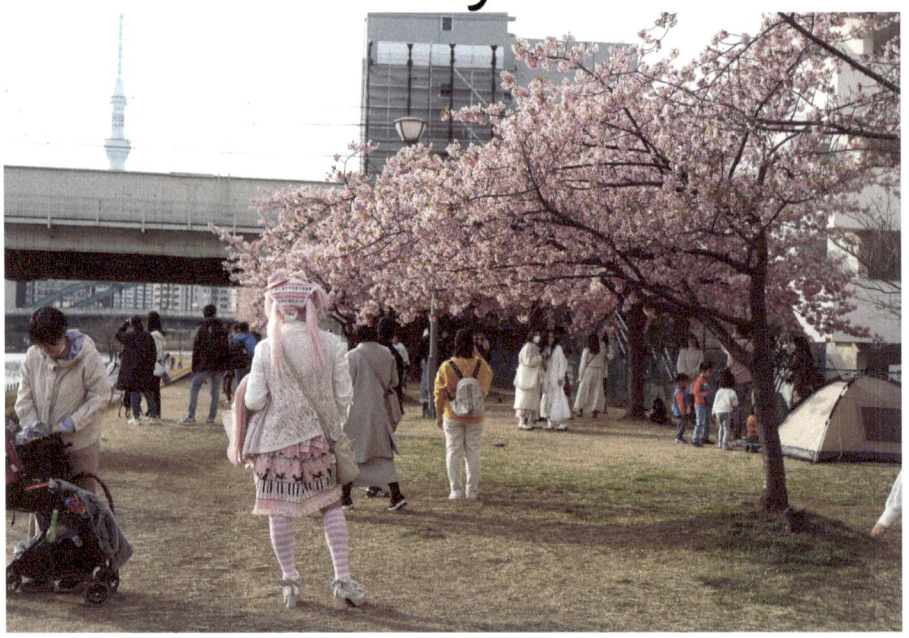

Edogawa City, Tokyo Japan

Description:

People frequently gather with friends, family, and coworkers to celebrate and enjoy the beauty of the cherry blossoms.

Hirai Cherry Blossom

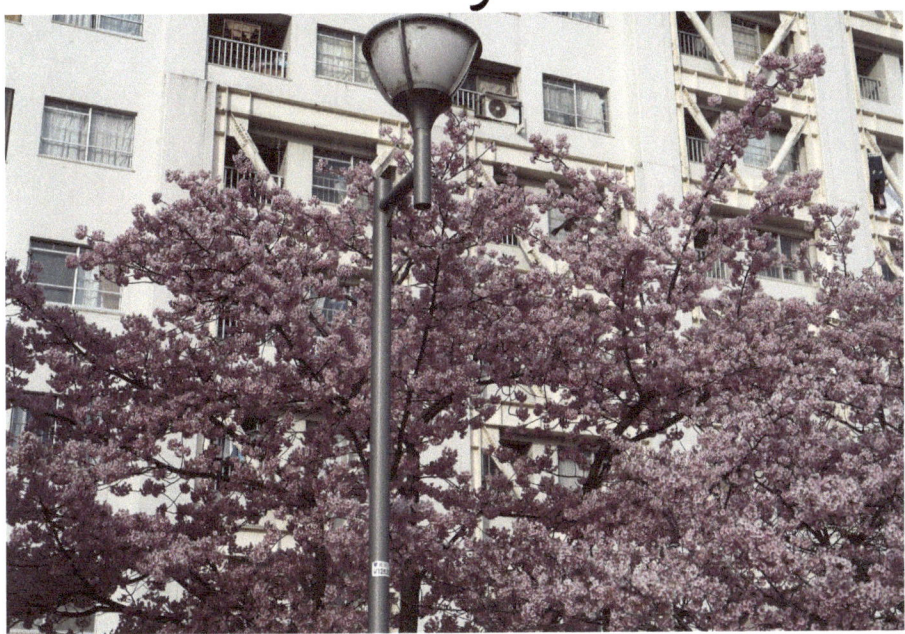

Edogawa City, Tokyo Japan

Description:
Ueno Park, Shinjuku Gyoen, and Chidorigafuchi are also popular areas.

Hirai Cherry Blossom

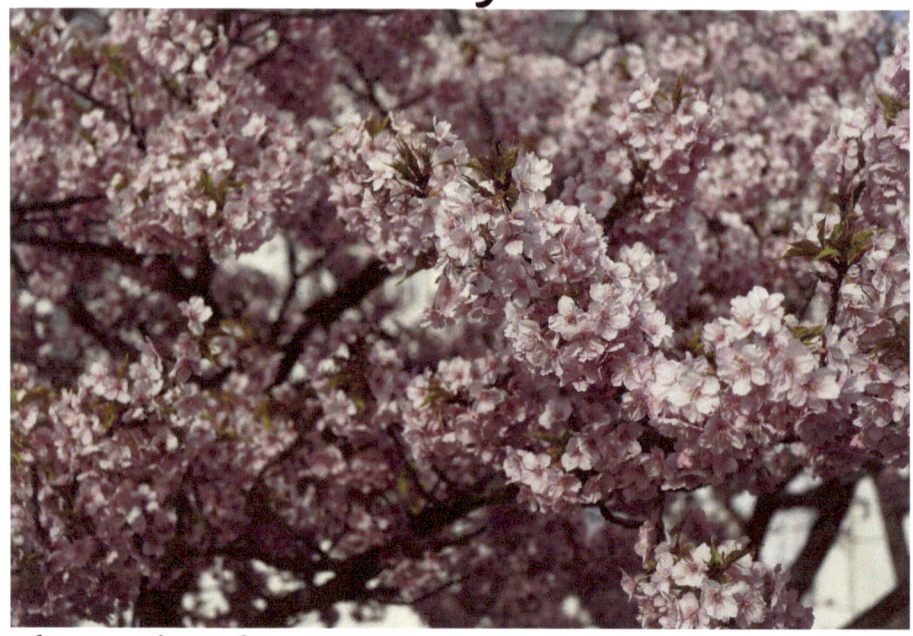

Edogawa City, Tokyo Japan

Description:

For generations, the Hirai Cherry Blossoms have been a popular hanami destination.

Hirai Cherry Blossom

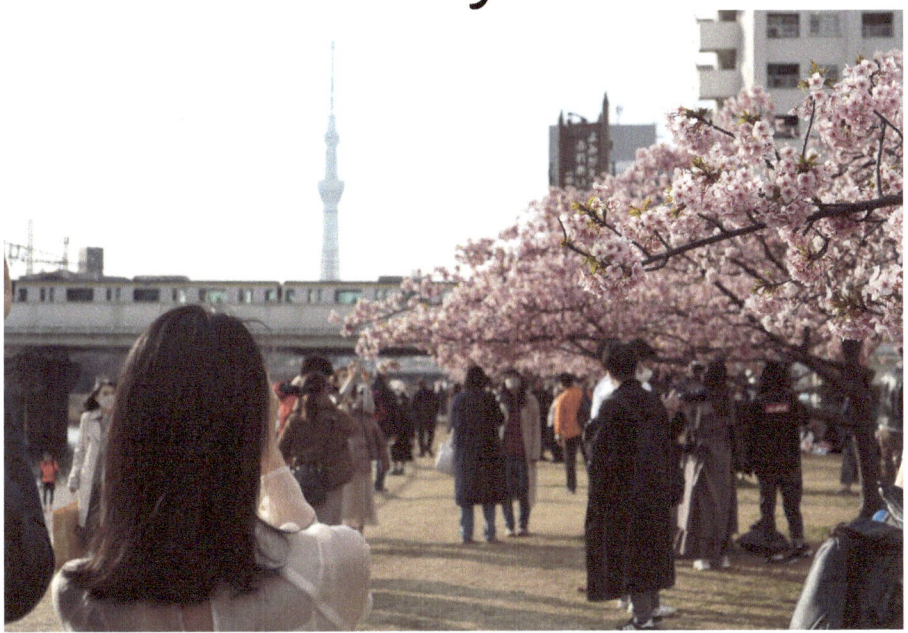

Edogawa City, Tokyo Japan

Description:

Sakura is the Japanese word for cherry blossom, and it's a popular girl's name in Japan.

Hirai Cherry Blossom

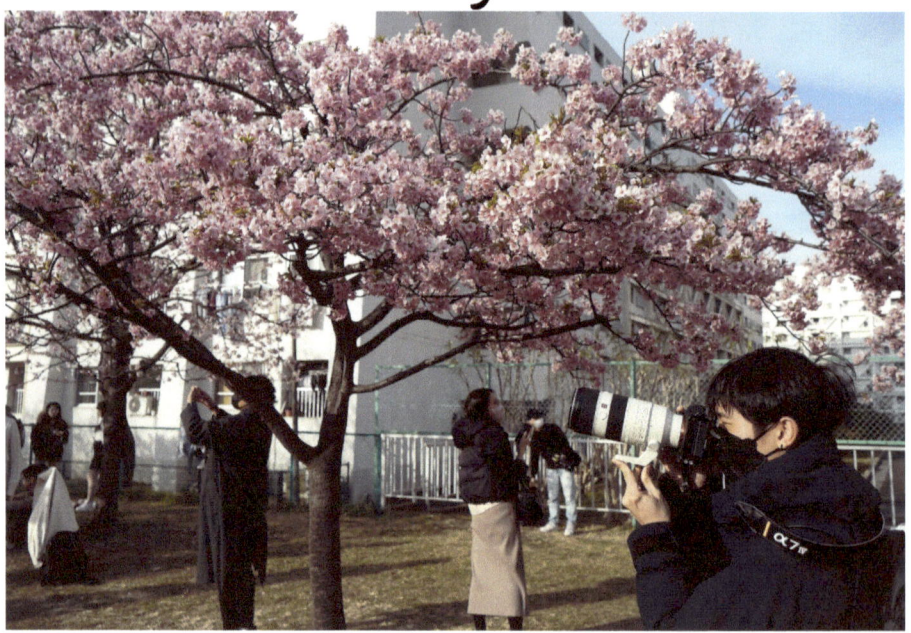

Edogawa City, Tokyo Japan
Description:
The contrast of the pink petals against the blue sky is stunning.

Hirai Cherry Blossom

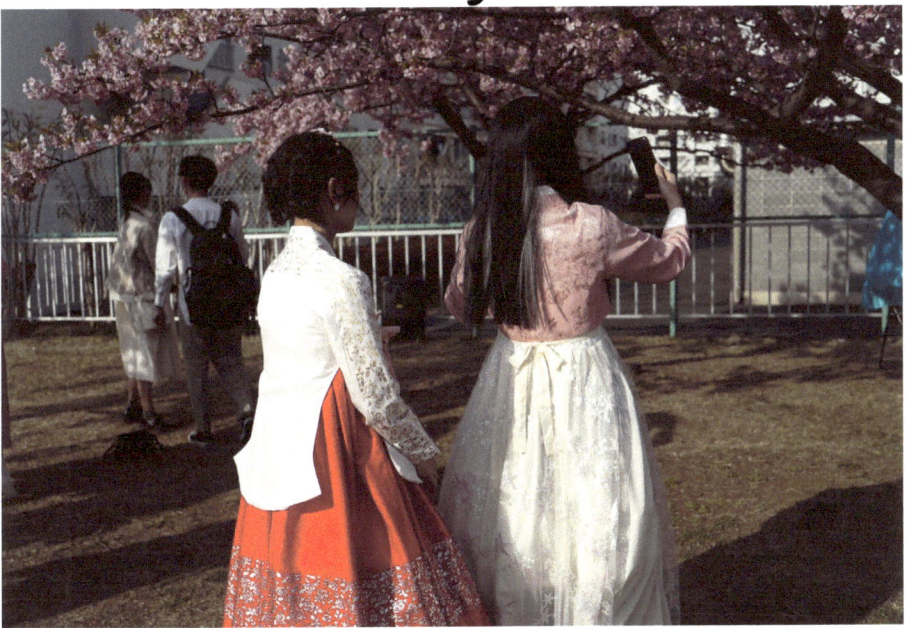

Edogawa City, Tokyo Japan

Description:

The beauty of the Hirai Cherry Blossoms can be appreciated by people of all ages and backgrounds.

Hirai Cherry Blossom

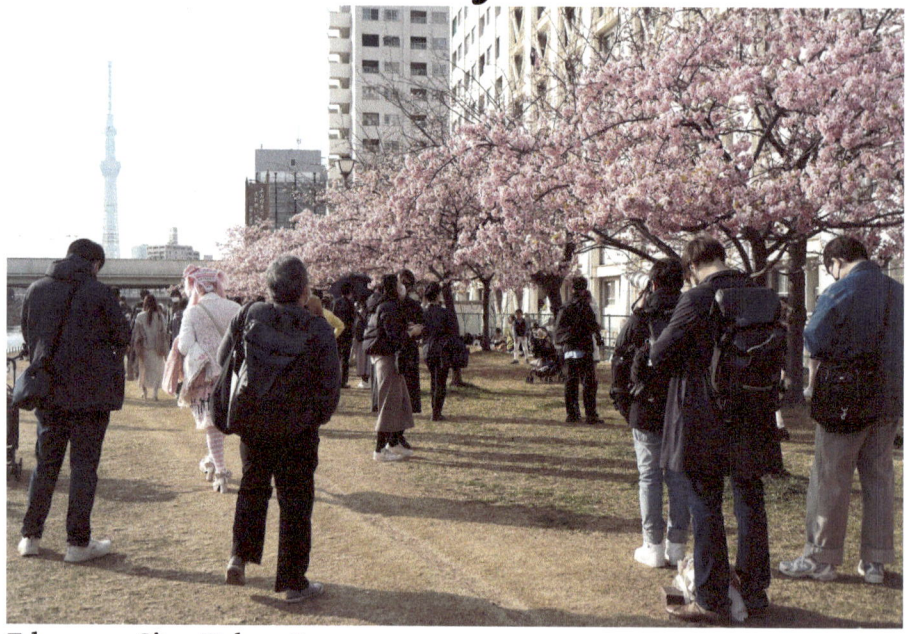

Edogawa City, Tokyo Japan

Description:

The Hirai Cherry Blossoms are a must-see for anyone visiting Tokyo in the spring, whether alone or with a group.

Hirai Cherry Blossom

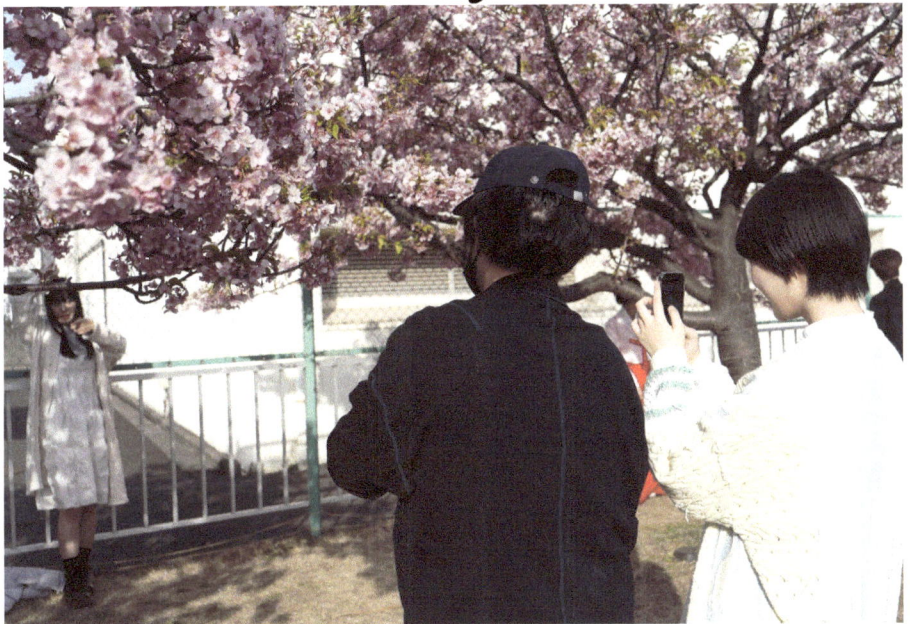

Edogawa City, Tokyo Japan

Description:

The Hirai Cherry Blossoms serve as a reminder of nature's beauty and wonder, as well as the importance of taking the time to appreciate it.

Hirai Cherry Blossom

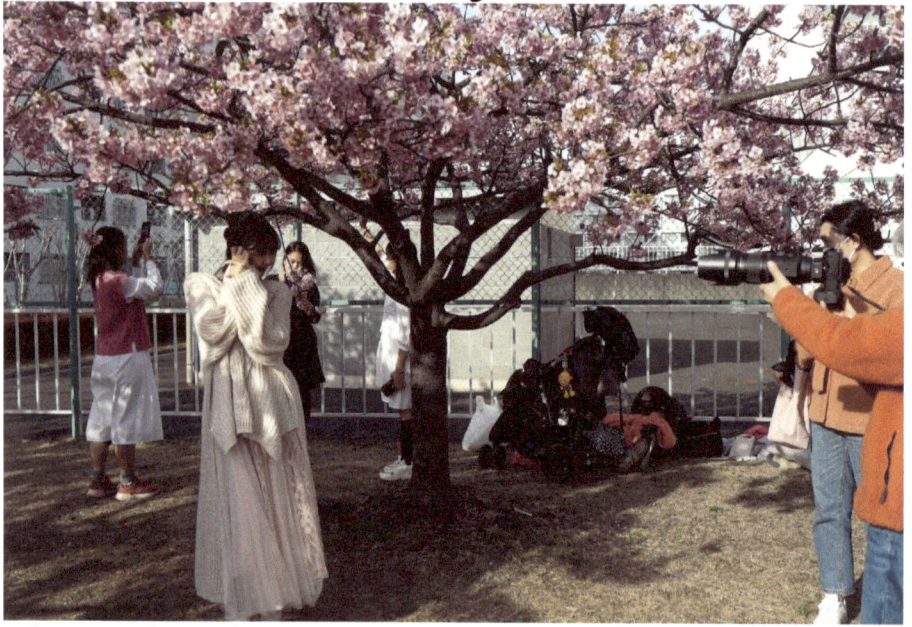

Edogawa City, Tokyo Japan

Description:
Cherry blossom season in Japan also coincides with the start of the school year, adding to the excitement and anticipation.

Hirai Cherry Blossom

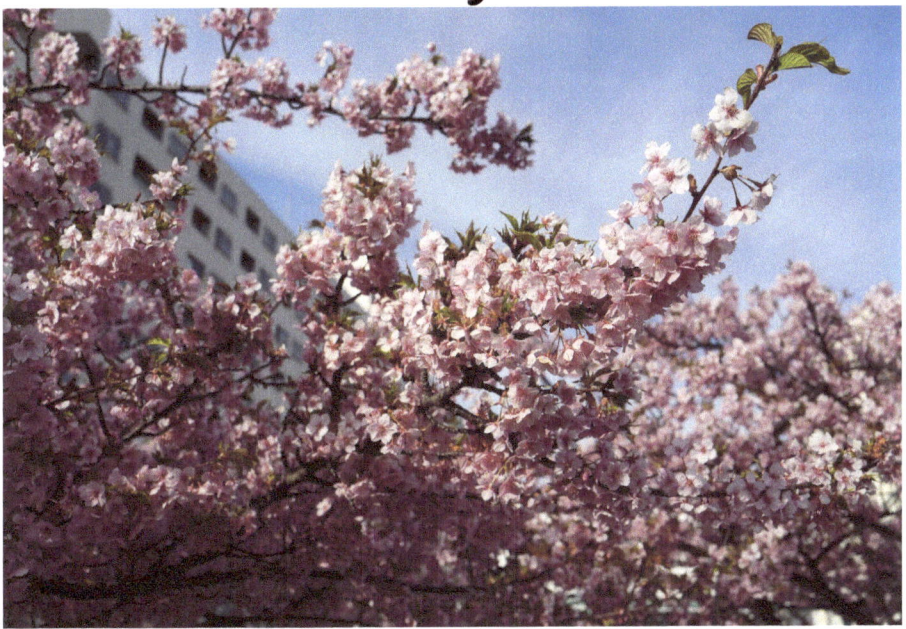

Edogawa City, Tokyo Japan

Description:

The Hirai neighborhood is a peaceful and serene retreat from Tokyo's hectic city life.

Hirai Cherry Blossom

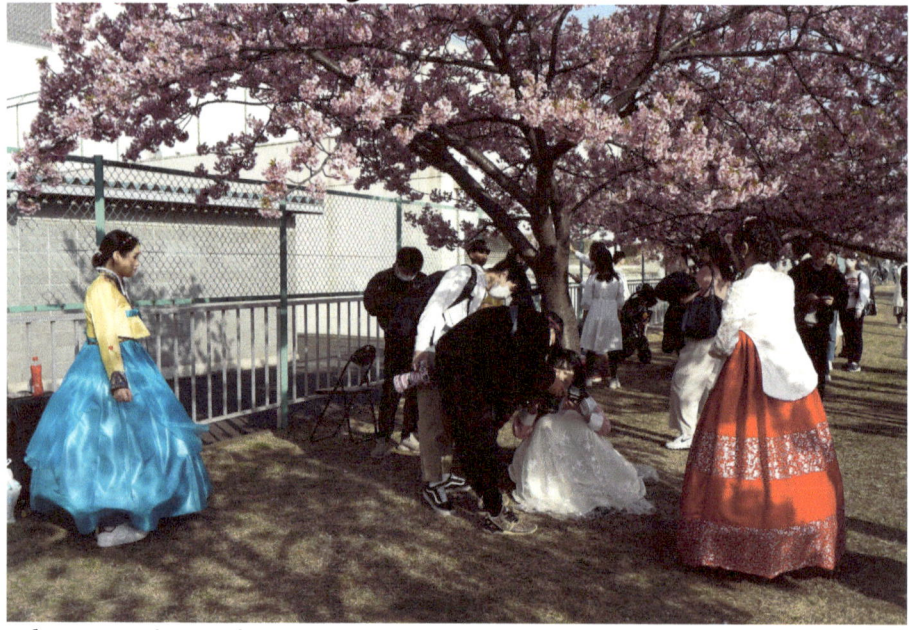

Edogawa City, Tokyo Japan

Description:
Cherry blossom viewing is a centuries-old Japanese tradition with roots in the imperial court and samurai culture.

Hirai Cherry Blossom

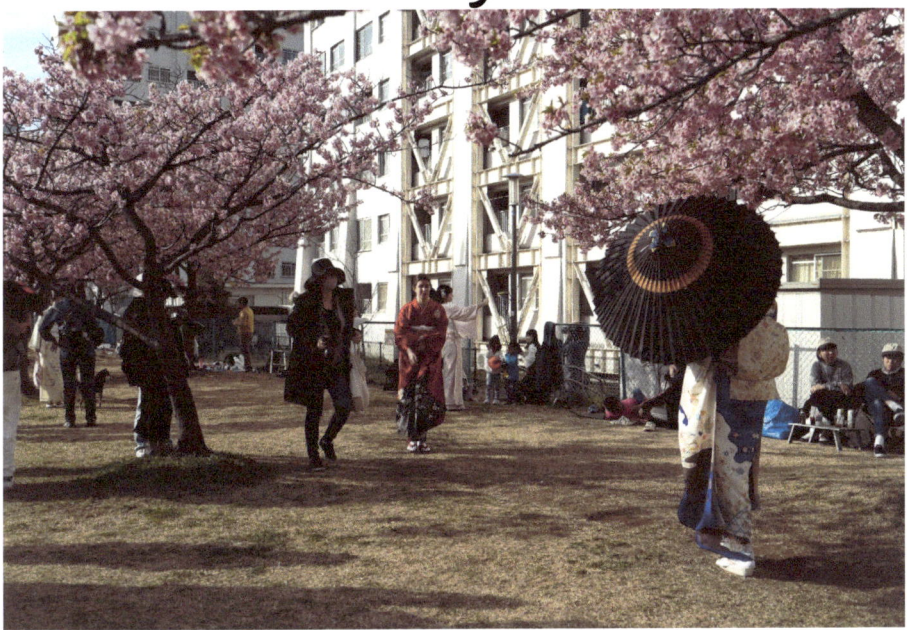

Edogawa City, Tokyo Japan

Description:

It is not unusual for visitors to hanami to wear traditional Japanese clothing, such as kimonos.

Hirai Cherry Blossom

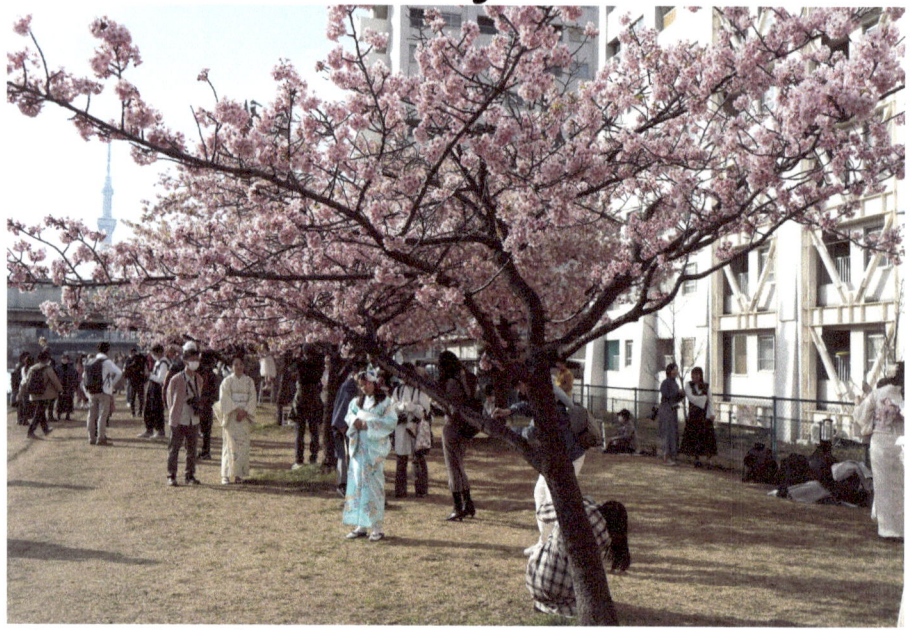

Edogawa City, Tokyo Japan

Description:
Many Japanese products and foods, such as sakura-flavored ice cream and sakura-themed stationery, are also inspired by cherry blossoms.

Hirai Cherry Blossom

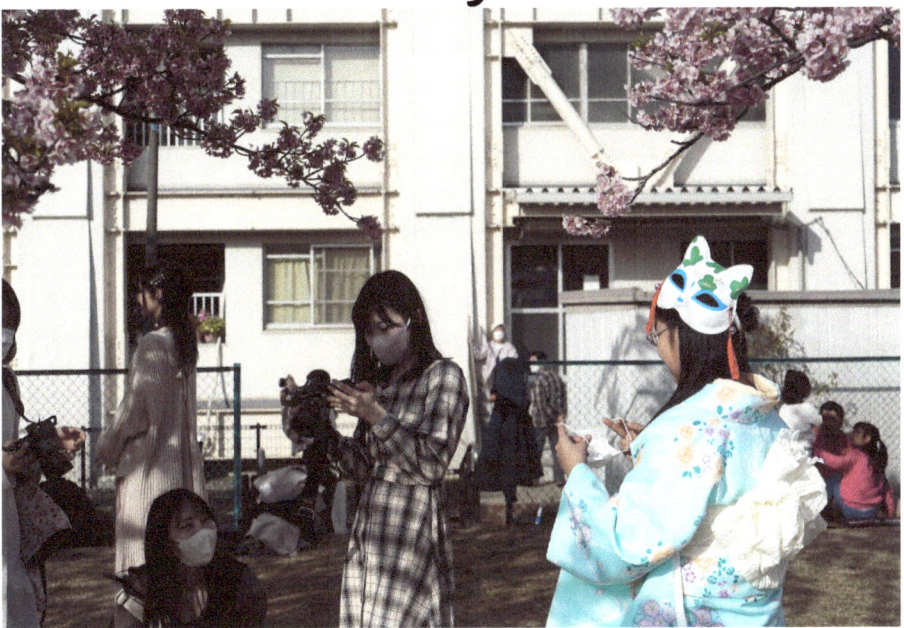

Edogawa City, Tokyo Japan

Description:
Many visitors take photos with the cherry blossoms as a backdrop, creating lasting memories of their visit.

Hirai Cherry Blossom

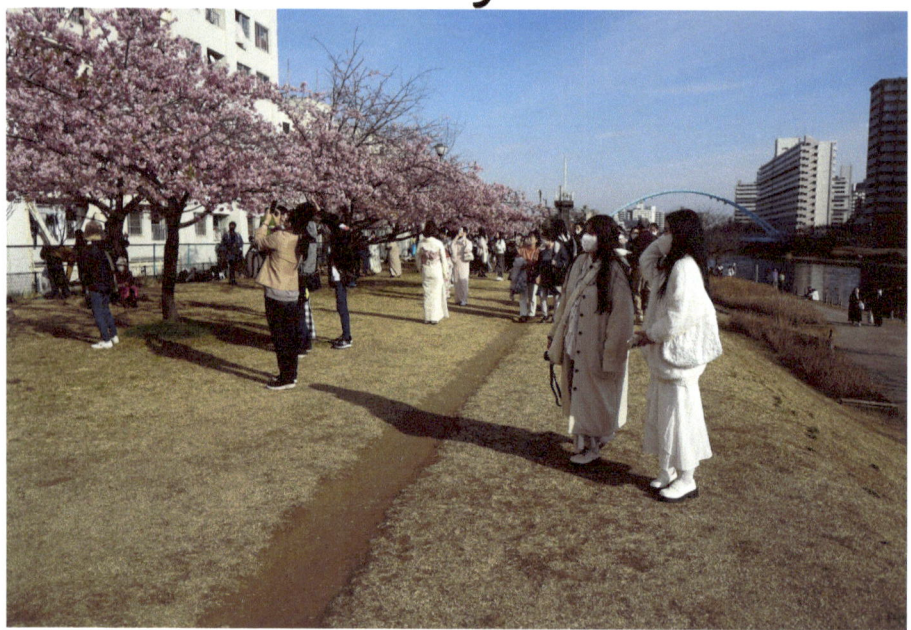

Edogawa City, Tokyo Japan

Description:
Many visitors bring picnic blankets, food, and drinks to enjoy while admiring the cherry blossoms.

Hirai Cherry Blossom

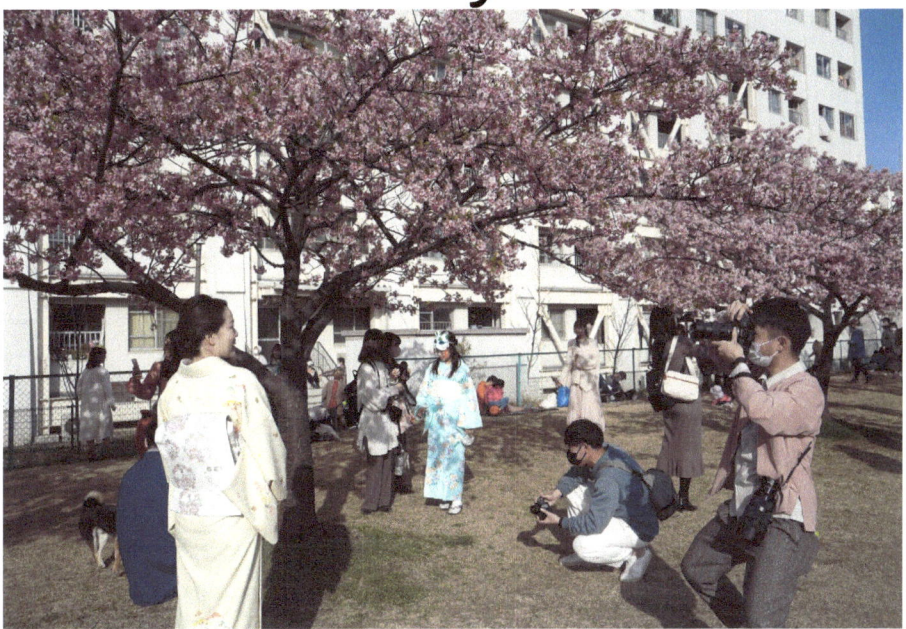

Edogawa City, Tokyo Japan

Description:
It's a truly unforgettable experience that will leave visitors with a lasting impression.

Hirai Cherry Blossom

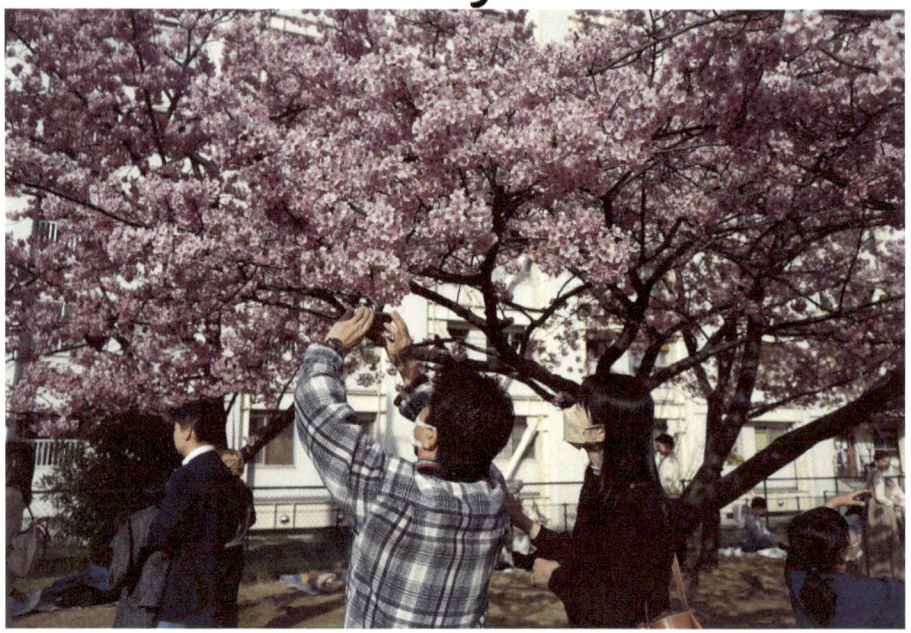

Edogawa City, Tokyo Japan

Description:

The Hirai Cherry Blossoms are also a popular destination for couples looking for a romantic stroll and to enjoy each other's company.

Hirai Cherry Blossom

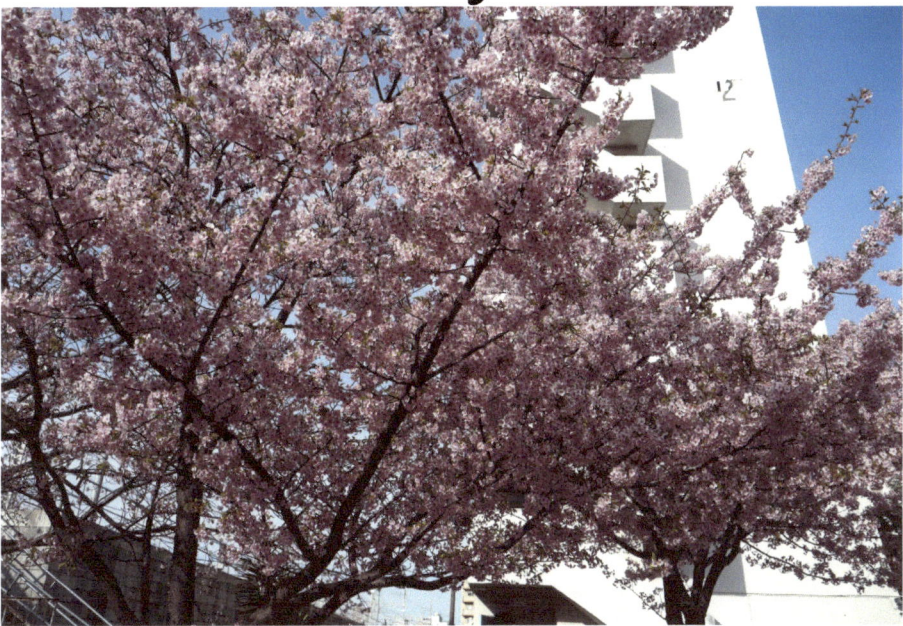

Edogawa City, Tokyo Japan

Description:

Cherry blossoms come in many different varieties, each with its own distinct beauty.

Hirai Cherry Blossom

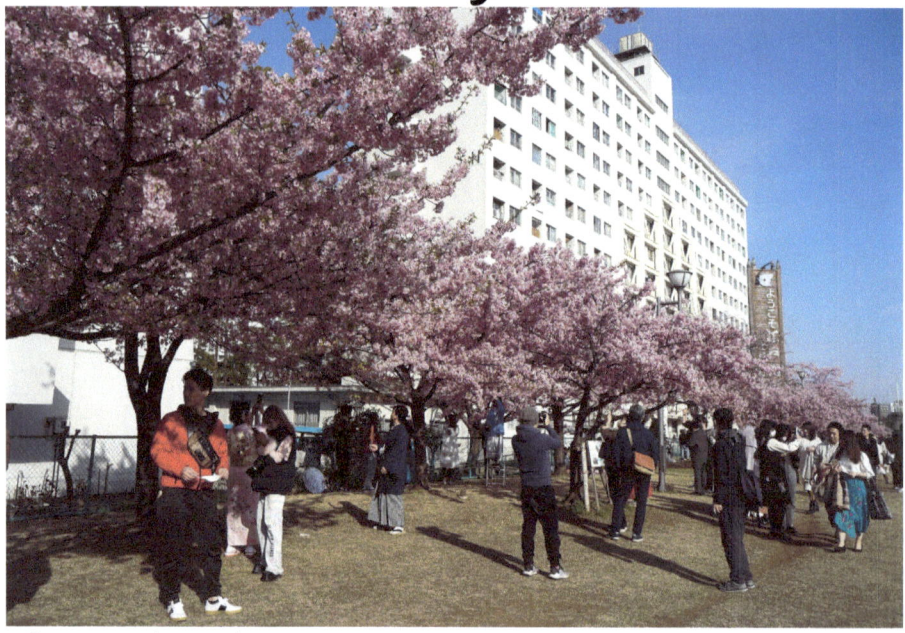

Edogawa City, Tokyo Japan

Description:
The Hirai area can get quite crowded during cherry blossom season, but the atmosphere is always lively and fun.

Tokyo Paul's Other Books

Title:
Japan Info Guide: Tips & Photos For An Amazing Experience in Japan!

Description:
This book is your ticket to the most current, relevant recommendations on what to see and skip and what undiscovered gems are waiting for you. I share my years of experience traveling and living in Japan with you. With your dependable travel buddy, see more than a hundred temples in Kyoto, unwind in a hot spring strewn over the island, and savor the diversity of Japan's delicious foods. Start your tour immediately, enjoy my high-quality photos, and get to the heart of Japan with me.

Book Cover:

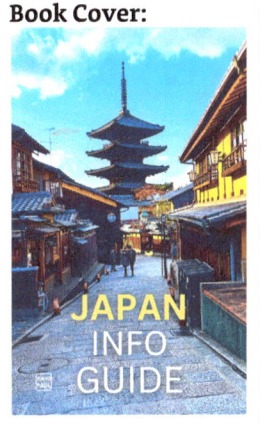

Tokyo Paul's Other Books

Title:
Japan Photobook 2023

Description:
This wonderful Japan Photobook contains more than 75 pages of breathtaking images from my YouTube Japan travels. You can visit the same locations because they are well-marked! Discover the gorgeous towns and sites of Japan through breathtaking photographs. Let the stunning cityscapes, festival scenes, cherry blossoms, and illuminations take you there! This book includes images of excellent quality and resolution. Every city, including Akihabara, Asakusa, Yokohama, Ueno, Ginza, Hakone, Nikko, etc., has a breathtaking atmosphere. This fantastic book beautifully captures Japan's incredible energy and way of life.

Book Cover:

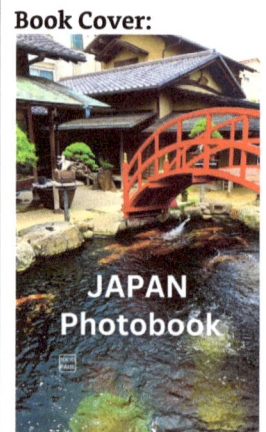

Tokyo Paul's Other Books

Title:
Japan and Its Famous Regional Foods & Things

Description:
This comprehensive guidebook explores Japan's rich culture and history through its 47 prefectures. From the bustling streets of Tokyo to the tranquil landscapes of Okinawa, discover each region's unique characteristics and famous attractions. From the historical temples and shrines in Kyoto to the renowned seafood of Hokkaido, this book delves deep into the heart of Japan, detailing the famous regional specialties, delicious local cuisines, and traditional customs of each prefecture. With detailed information, this book is perfect for travelers planning their next trip to Japan and those wanting to deepen their understanding of Japan.

Book Cover:

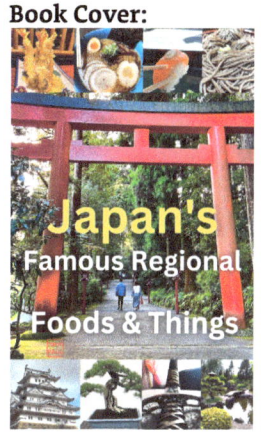

Tokyo Paul's Other Books

Title:
Tokyo Info Guide: Tips & Photos For Traveling in Japan

Description:
This book is your best travel companion for discovering Tokyo's lively and diverse cityscape. This thorough guidebook offers in-depth details on the city's history, culture, prominent attractions, helpful advice for navigating the city like a local, and a map of the most popular train line. A valuable tool for first-time tourists, the guidebook also offers essential information on the Japanese language. The Tokyo Guidebook is the ideal travel companion for anyone visiting Tokyo, Japan.

Book Cover:

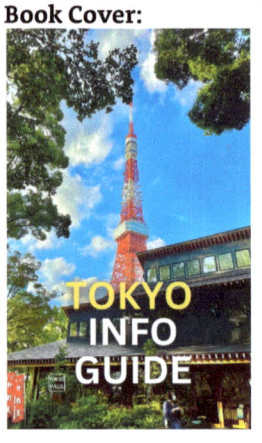

Tokyo Paul's Other Books

Title:
Japan Trip Planner (Journal) Kindle Edition

Description:
Compact Size: 6 inches by 9 inches
Ample space for writing notes for 10-15 plus trips
Included Sections:
• 100 Must-See Recommendations, 75 Places & 25 Seasonal Events by Popularity
• Budget Log Section
• Checklists: Pre-trip Checklist, Foods Checklist

Book Cover:

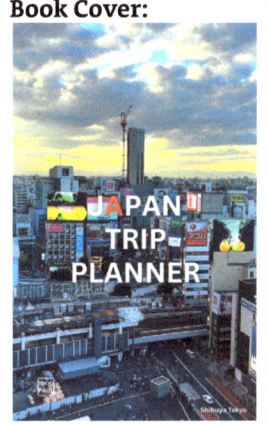

About the Author

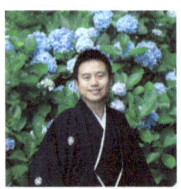

Tokyo Paul is an Asian American who has lived in Japan for over seven years. He's lived everywhere, from Osaka to Nagasaki to Toyama to Tokyo in Japan. He enjoys live-streaming videos on YouTube on his channel. He is an avid sushi fan and goes to his favorite sushi restaurant Sushiro every week. He is also on Twitter, Instagram, and Facebook if you wish to follow him for more information about Japan.

Thank you for finishing this book with me. I'm Tokyo Paul. Consider checking me out on YouTube, search Tokyo Paul to watch my videos about Japan, or any other social media platform such as Facebook, Instagram, and Twitter. Safe journeys, everyone!

The End

www.ingramcontent.com/pod-product-compliance
Lightning Source LLC
Chambersburg PA
CBHW040321220526
45473CB00009B/2516